Shaping a Woman's Soul

Books by Judith Couchman

Shaping a Woman's Soul

Designing a Woman's Life

Designing a Woman's Life Bible Study

Lord, Please Help Me to Change

Lord, Have You Forgotten Me?

Why Is Her Life Better Than Mine?

If I'm So Good, Why Don't I Act That Way?

Getting a Grip on Guilt

Compilations by Judith Couchman

Loving God with All Your Heart

A Very Present Help

Shaping a Woman's Soul

Daily Devotions to Calm Your Spirit and Lead You into God's Presence

ZondervanPublishingHouse
Grand Rapids, Michigan

A Division of HarperCollins*Publishers*

JUDITH COUCHMAN

Shaping a Woman's Soul
© 1996 by Judy C. Couchman

Requests for information should be addressed to:

ZondervanPublishingHouse
Grand Rapids, Michigan 49530

Library of Congress Cataloging-in-Publication Data

Couchman, Judith, 1953–
Shaping a woman's soul: daily devotions to calm your spirit and lead you into God's presence / Judith Couchman.
p. cm.
ISBN: 0-310-20517-4 (pbk.)
1. Women—Prayer-books and devotions—English. I. Title.
BV4844.C68 1996
242'.643—dc 20 96-23831
CIP

All Scripture quotations, unless otherwise indicated, are taken from the *Holy Bible: New International Version*®. NIV®. Copyright © 1973, 1978, 1984 by International Bible Society. Used by permission of Zondervan Publishing House. All rights reserved.

Verses marked KJV are from the King James Version of the Bible.

All rights reserved. No part of this publication may be reproduced, stored in a retrieval system, or transmitted in any form or by any means—electronic, mechanical, photocopy, recording, or any other—except for brief quotations in printed reviews, without the prior permission of the publisher.

Published in association with the literary agency of Alive Communications, Inc., 1465 Kelly Johnson Boulevard, Suite 320, Colorado Springs, CO 80920.

Interior design by Sherri L. Hoffman

Printed in the United States of America

96 97 98 99 00 01 02 03 /❖ DH/ 10 9 8 7 6 5 4 3 2

For Opal Mary Storey Couchman,
my mother and best friend.
In my youth you taught me to grow the soul
and believed I'd write about it someday.
For this and your unconditional love,
every book of mine could be dedicated to you.

CONTENTS

ACKNOWLEDGMENTS

I offer a deep and heartfelt thanks to Zondervan and my editor, Ann Spangler, for believing that another "soul book" could be fresh and inviting—and for taking on me, an author new to their publishing ventures. Ann, along with Rachel Boers, deserves kudos for helping me shape this manuscript into an appealing format with readable content.

A bouquet of thanks also goes to the literary agency Alive Communications and my agent, Greg Johnson, for lifting paperwork and contract negotiations off my shoulders and placing them in capable hands.

I am also grateful to my niece Melissa Honeywell for her research assistance, which pulled me through tight deadlines, and to the friends and family members who consistently cheered me on. Thank you to Mary Brosa, Deena Davis, Nancy Lemons, Beth Lueders, and Susan Pannell for being faithful "phone friends" when we couldn't get together. And thanks to Barb Mortensen and Shirley Honeywell, who love and support a "crazy writer" sister and express pride in my books. I pray we keep growing closer as the years pass.

As always, I'm indebted to my prayer team. Along with my mother, Opal Couchman, her friend Mae Lammers, and my sister Shirley Honeywell, these steadfast and creative friends prayed for me and this book's message: Charette Barta, Win Couchman, Madalene

Harris, Karen Hilt, and Nancy Lemons. From their close-up and realistic examples, I have learned about shaping the soul.

Most of all, I'm indebted to my mother. Without her unconditional love, interest, support, and prayers, I probably wouldn't write at all. Mom, thanks for being my biggest fan and dearest, deepest friend. I'll love you forever.

INTRODUCTION

LIVING

Believing That the Inside Counts

A wonderful Saviour is Jesus my Lord,
A wonderful Saviour to me;
He hideth my soul in the cleft of the rock,
Where rivers of pleasure I see.

A wonderful Saviour is Jesus my Lord,
He taketh my burden away;
He holdeth me up and I shall not be moved,
He giveth me strength day by day.

With numberless blessings each moment He crowns,
And, filled with His fullness divine,
I sing in my rapture, "O glory to God
For such a redeemer as mine!"

He hideth my soul in the cleft of the rock,
That shadows a dry, thirsty land;
He hideth my life in the depth of His love,
And covers me there with His hand,
And covers me there with His hand.

"He Hideth My Soul"
by Fanny J. Crosby and William J. Kirkpatrick

I rolled over in bed, tangled myself in a quilt, and stared at the ceiling. Outside my hotel room, the ocean roared its welcome, but I couldn't hear it. Nor did I care. A bolted door, shuttered windows, a low-droning television felt fine by me. I didn't want to hear. I didn't want to think. I didn't want to be.

I hadn't taken a vacation in several years, so this seaside inn was supposed to be my port of refuge, my time to play and relax. Instead, it served as an emotional prison, a place to shut out the madding crowd and wrestle the chaos within. At a time when my life and work climbed to a peak, I felt utterly miserable. Depleted. Washed up on a lonely sandbar.

What's wrong with me? I questioned. *Why do I always wind up this way?*

Unfortunately I'd felt this mind-numbing pain several times before. After periods of intense work and accomplishment, I'd collapse in a depressed heap, unable to feel, think, or do much of anything. And I didn't understand why. Even though I'd been spiritually aware for years, I hadn't yet learned to care for the woman within. I'd devoted abundant time to acquiring external rewards and possessions, neglecting the condition of my soul.

In recent years, a plethora of soul books have hit the bookstores and sold in big numbers. It's no wonder. Our culture spins at a death-defying pace, and we yearn for a simpler lifestyle, for something to fill our empty hearts. Christians are no exception. Though our voices sing "No man careth for my soul like Jesus," our lives can belie what we profess. Not because we're traitors or hypocrites, but because we can't—or don't or won't—take time to "be still."

Women, especially, struggle with slowing down and looking within. Traditionally we cast ourselves as the caretakers, the ones who ensure that everybody and everything runs smoothly. We are the need meeters and self-sacrificers. If we are "good" wives, mothers, bosses, employees, and friends, then husbands, children, employees, employers, and friends swallow up our time. Besides, nurturing ourselves sounds selfish and vaguely antibiblical.

Interestingly, the opposite is true. Jesus asked, "What good will it be for a man if he gains the whole world, yet forfeits his soul? Or what can a man give in exchange for his soul?" I'm certain the Master intended these questions for women too. For to be wholly human and fully alive is to taste the divine, call up the Holy Spirit's resources within, and live from the inside out. According to Jesus, our most important life task—indeed, the key to living—is plumping up and shaping the soul.

After reviewing several recent soul books, I still desired a practical, accessible book that would give me a day-by-day look at spiritual development and include everyday examples. But most of all, a book that doesn't neglect the heavenly Father who lavishes gifts on his children yet creates moral instructions for them. With *Shaping a Woman's Soul* I hope I've created that book—a thought-provoking experience for women who long to develop their inner selves, to find rest and encouragement in God.

This is also a book written from personal experience, from the musings and lessons of a soul-development journey I'm still embarked upon, probably for the rest of my life. Since that day at a Canadian inn a few years ago, God has prompted me to slow down, change course, and explore putting his kingdom above all else. I'm learning about fattening the soul first, then moving into the world with joy, fulfillment, and spiritual influence. In other words, purposefully enlarging the soul rather than unwittingly withering it with busyness and self-gratification.

This is an ancient yet still radical approach for my generation. I pray it becomes a life-changing message for you.

PART ONE

HIDING

Pulling Away and Within

O safe to the Rock that is higher than I,
My soul in its conflicts and sorrows would fly;
So sinful, so weary, Thine Thine, would I be;
Thou blest "Rock of Ages," I'm hiding in Thee.

Hiding in Thee, Hiding in Thee,
Thou Blest "Rock of Ages," I'm hiding in Thee.

In the calm of the noontide, in sorrow's lone hour,
In times when temptation casts o'er me its power;
In the tempests of life, on its wide, heaving sea,
Thou blest "Rock of Ages," I'm hiding in Thee.

Hiding in Thee, Hiding in Thee,
Thou Blest "Rock of Ages," I'm hiding in Thee.

"Hiding in Thee"
by William O. Cushing and Ira D. Sankey

"On Father's Day, 1982, I came home from church, locked myself in the bedroom and refused to come out," recalls Alice Slaikeu Lawhead in her book *The Lie of the Good Life.*

"I wouldn't come out for a toddler banging on the door, for a baby who needed to nurse, or for a confused husband who just wanted to know if I was okay.

"Okay? No, I wasn't okay.

"Because life—my life—wasn't turning out as I'd expected. All my assumptions were being challenged; my disappointment was overwhelming. My dreams were dying, one by one. And that being the case, I didn't see any reason why I should come out of the bedroom. At all. Ever."[1]

Alice eventually left the bedroom, but her story makes a good point. Sometimes we just need to hide.

Unfortunately, most of us ignore this need until life grows overwhelming and hiding out turns into a traumatic, last-ditch attempt to save our sanity. Then the baby screams louder, the toddler bangs on the door harder, the confused husband turns angry, and we feel guilty. Shouldn't we be able to keep up, to continue pitching as long as everybody and everything needs us? If we feel like hiding, aren't we weak-willed or irresponsible?

No. To feel like hiding is to be human, to recognize the soul's desire to pull away and within, to respond to a need for replenishment. The problem is, we don't hide often enough. If we practiced a periodic hiding, a repeated running away to God—often just for moments, sometimes for hours or days—we'd be less susceptible to letting the daily grind pulverize us.

"You are my hiding place," declared the psalmist to God. "You will protect me from trouble and surround me with songs of deliverance." And the Lord replied, "I will instruct you and teach you in the way you should go; I will counsel you and watch over you."

The Lord doesn't shame or chastise us for wanting to hide. He says, "Come to me. I will nurture and fill you. When you lock away with me, for that brief time the world will go away. I am the rock, your hiding place."

So why refuse the invitation? Why delay? You can proclaim with the psalmist, "You are my hiding place." You can hide away today.

TURNING INSIDE OUT

Rediscovering That Soul Matters

To you, O LORD, I lift up my soul;
in you I trust, O my God. . . .
Show me your ways, O LORD,
teach me your paths;
guide me in your truth and teach me,
for you are God my Savior,
and my hope is in you all day long. . . .
Search me, O God, and know my heart;
test me and know my anxious thoughts.
See if there is any offensive way in me,
and lead me in the way everlasting.

—Psalm 25:1–2, 4–5; 139:23–24

As a young man, the famous photographer Ansel Adams played the piano quite well. However, once at a party Adams performed Chopin's F Major Nocturne in a less-than-glowing manner.

"In some strange way my right hand started off in F-sharp major and my left hand behaved well in F major," he recalled. "I could not bring them together. I went through the entire nocturne with my hands separated by a half-step."

The next day, another guest complimented him: "You never missed a wrong note!"[2]

If we feel as though we're playing wrong notes, if no matter how hard we try, we're internally askew, it's time to ask, "What have I done for my soul lately?" Most likely the answer will be, "Not much."

When we neglect the soul, it devises ways to tell us. We feel restless and disconnected. Nothing satisfies and we ache inside. We try working, shopping, eating, cleaning, creating, lovemaking, or socializing, but these don't quell the inner throb. We run to whatever provides a quick fix, whatever keeps us busy, forgetting the remedy is spiritual, not physical, and only a half-step away into the soul.

Psychologist Larry Crabb says, "An aching soul is evidence not of neurosis or spiritual immaturity, but of realism."[3] And reality dictates that if we don't care for the soul, growing and shaping it in God's image, life turns unceasingly flat. We wind up like King Solomon, who complained, "I have seen all the things that are done under the sun; all of them are meaningless, a chasing after the wind."

But how, exactly, do we grow and shape the soul?

There are various methods—many are described in this book—but each way leads to the same destination. Soul development means periodically slowing down, hiding away, and replenishing the person within. It clears the mind, opens the heart, molds the will, revives the spirit. But most of all, soul time teaches us to live from the inside out rather than on the surface. It centers and transforms us, equipping us to live fully and graciously. It hands us the gift of meaning.

For Christians, soul work wraps itself in a relationship with God: loving, following, and obeying him. In turn it rewards us with the fruit of his Spirit: love, joy, peace, patience, kindness, goodness, faithfulness, gentleness, self-control. Yet these aren't qualities designed just to make us feel good. Christ asks us to lavish them on the world—loving, giving, and serving as he did two thousand years ago.

So how do we begin?

By quieting ourselves before God. We can pray with the psalmist, "To you, O Lord, I lift up my soul. Show me your ways, teach me your paths; guide me in your truth," and he will help us rediscover that soul matters.

Lord, my heart cries out, "Life is meaningless!" I ache inside and long to fill the emptiness with something that lasts. I realize you are the only one who can truly satisfy me. Please show me your path to growing and shaping my soul.

THE STRONG TOWER

Where to Run Away from It All

> The LORD is my rock, my fortress and my deliverer;
> my God is my rock, in whom I take refuge.
> He is my shield and the horn of my salvation, my stronghold. . . .
> Therefore I will praise you among the nations,
> O LORD;
> I will sing praises to your name. . . .
> For you have been my refuge,
> a strong tower against the foe.
>
> —Psalm 18:2, 49; 61:3

Alice never could quite make out, in thinking it over afterwards, how it was that they began. All she remembers is, that they were running hand in hand, and the Queen went so fast that it was all she could do to keep up with her.

"And still the Queen kept crying, 'Faster! Faster!' but Alice felt she could not go faster, though she had no breath left to say so. The most curious part of the thing was, that the trees and the other things round them never changed their places at all. However fast they went, they never seemed to pass anything.

"Just as Alice was getting quite exhausted, they stopped. [She] looked around her in great surprise. 'Why, I do believe we've been under this tree the whole time! Everything's just as it was!'

"'Of course it is,' said the Queen. 'It takes all the running you can do, to keep in the same place. If you want to get somewhere else, you must run twice as fast as that!'"[4]

Like Alice and the Red Queen in *Through the Looking-Glass,* we are a generation of women bent on running. Hurry here. Scurry there. Sprint to the office. Hustle the kids. Run by the neighbor's. Dash through the store. So much running, yet it seems we're getting nowhere. So much running, we feel like running away.

Where did we learn that relentless running is a virtue? Certainly we have responsibilities; certainly we must keep them. But how much is too much? How long can we run before we implode? Often "too much" arrives sooner than expected, and without time off we can burn out on short notice.

But I have good news. It's all right, even necessary, to run away from it all.

God invites us to run to him and then stop running, to hide out in his strong tower away from the clamoring world. The psalmist remembered, "In my distress I called to the LORD; I cried to my God for help. From his temple he heard my voice; my cry came before him, into his ears. . . . He reached down from on high and took hold of me; he drew me out of deep waters."

We may not be drowning in deep waters, but God knows that running aground—or even running in circles—feels just as perilous and exhausting. So he listens for our call; he wants to answer. He prepares a table for us each day, a feast of delight. He swings open the door; he desires that we enter in. He's willing to protect us from the foe even when the enemy is our self-made busyness. He promises to replenish our souls.

The Lord looks and asks, "Who will come today?" He patiently listens but only hears the stampede of female feet running in the wrong direction. But still he waits.

God, I've been running and running, but I feel as if I'm getting nowhere. How I want to change! Beginning today, I will run to you and take refuge in your strong tower. I will sit at your table and feast on the delight of your presence.

UNDER HIS WINGS

Living Where the Shadow Falls

I call on you, O God, for you will answer me;
give ear to me and hear my prayer.
Show the wonder of your great love,
you who save by your right hand
those who take refuge in you from their foes. . . .
I long to dwell in your tent forever
and take refuge in the shelter of your wings.

—Psalm 17:6–7; 61:4

Last summer two birds took up housekeeping on my front porch, each in her own hanging pot of ivy. For several days I enjoyed watching them build nests one twig at a time. But the situation changed when the birds became expectant mothers.

After the eggs arrived, I couldn't step on the porch without both moms chirping with all their lung power. The cacophony grew so intense that I began using the back door, except to greet visitors or check the mailbox. Then after the babies hatched, the mother noise sounded so annoying that not even the cat would go near them. I stopped watering the plants in the hanging pots, preferring to buy new ones after the birds abandoned their nests.

The protective mama birds had successfully communicated their message: *Stay away from my children!* They took seriously their responsibility to guard and protect, to provide a safe haven until their young could fly.

It feels slightly odd to compare God to noisy birds, but Scripture speaks of the Lord's pinions, of hiding in the shadow of his wings. While escaping the clutches of King Saul, David the shepherd begged God, "Keep me as the apple of your eye; hide me in the shadow of your wings." David wanted God's eagle eye on him, the Lord's great wings hovering over him for guidance and protection. He needed a safe place when, tired and afraid, he couldn't face the world.

I envision David singing in the black night:

> Under His wings, I am safely abiding;
> Though the night deepens and tempests are wild,
> Still I can trust Him, I know He will keep me;
> He has redeemed me and I am His child.

Likewise, when we pull away to refurbish the soul, we can imagine the Lord's pinions spread over us, his fierce love staving off intruders. But unlike the fleeing David, we don't need to wait until danger lurks nearby. We can hide under God's wings at any time. In the mornings, in the midst of a hectic day, when we're in pain, when we're weary, we can take refuge under his wings until once again it's our time to fly.

> Under His wings, Under His wings,
> Who from His love can sever?
> Under His wings my soul shall abide,
> Safely abide forever.[5]

Dear Sheltering One, remind me that you offer a safe place to hide, away from the enemies of my soul. Teach me to nestle in the shadow of your wings. Hover over me, protect me, nourish me, until once again I'm ready to fly.

SOLITUDE

Venturing into the Aloneness

My soul finds rest in God alone;
    my salvation comes from him.
He alone is my rock and my salvation;
    he is my fortress, I will never be shaken. . . .
Find rest, O my soul, in God alone;
    my hope comes from him.
He alone is my rock and my salvation;
    he is my fortress, I will not be shaken.

—Psalm 62:1–2, 5–6

Twenty years ago Annie Dillard moved to an island on Puget Sound. She lived alone and explained, "I came here to study the hard things—rock mountain and salt sea—and to temper my spirit on their edges. 'Teach me thy ways, O Lord' is, like all prayers, a rash one, and one I cannot but recommend."

For two years Annie asked herself hard questions about life and the will of God. She described her living quarters as "one room, one enormous window, one cat, one spider, and one person." Then she admitted, "But I am hollow."[6]

With those tacked-on but poignant words, Annie exposed what we may fear: if we spend time alone, be it hours or days or years, we might peer inside ourselves only to discover we're empty.

Solitude can frighten us if we don't grasp its spiritual significance. But if we squarely face ourselves and offer up the emptiness to God, this aloneness can forge a path to inner joy. Teresa of Avila of ancient times advised, "Settle yourself in solitude and you will come upon Him in yourself."[7] When invited, God fills empty souls with himself, and in his presence "is fullness of joy." With this joy, our solitude tastes sweet, for we're passing time with the attentive lover of our souls.

In 1670 the poet Mary Mollineux exclaimed, "How sweet is harmless solitude! How can its joys control? Tumults and noise may not intrude, to interrupt the soul."[8] Her words could aptly describe a person who enters into aloneness and there discovers God.

Yet this joyful solitude may not arrive swiftly or easily. This joy must be hoped for, prayed for, and allowed the luxury of time to infuse the soul. It may require repeated ventures into aloneness before it manifests itself. God does not arrive and perform on demand. He waits until our hearts are ready. Often this joy follows a pouring out of the soul's sins and concerns to him.

Still, solitude is to be desired and pursued. Paul wrote to the Roman Christians, "May the God of hope fill you with all joy and peace as you trust in him, so that you may overflow with hope by the power of the Holy Spirit." When our solitary time ends, this hope carries us through the busy and uncertain days ahead.

With my busy schedule, when can I carve out time for solitude? Please create small miracles so from time to time, I can be alone with you, dear God. Take away any fear of being alone. I want to rejoice in my emptiness, because it means I can fill up with you. Help me to say, "I will not fear the solitude, for there I can find God."

HIDING YOUR HEART

Savoring Moments of Inner Retreat

Hear my voice when I call, O LORD;
    be merciful to me and answer me.
My heart says of you, "Seek his face!"
    Your face, LORD, I will seek.
I am still confident of this:
    I will see the goodness of the LORD
    in the land of the living.
Wait for the LORD;
    be strong and take heart
    and wait for the LORD.

—Psalm 27:7–8, 13–14

With a baby on one hip and a toddler in tow, Dee laughed and asked, "Find time to wait on God? These kids won't even let me go to the bathroom by myself!"

On one level or another, most of us can empathize with my friend. With or without children, it's hard to arrange time to be alone. But solitude isn't the only way to develop a soul life or to practice the presence of God. We can create moments of inner retreat—times throughout the day when we turn soul-ward and

God-ward—whether we're working or creating or exercising or playing.

For example, Brother Lawrence praised God while he cooked meals in a monastery kitchen. As a young man, the preacher A. W. Tozer worked in a tire factory with "worshipful tears" in his eyes. I feel close to the Creator while gardening or mowing the lawn. A friend of mine senses God's presence when she shapes clay on a potter's wheel. A few years ago I met a woman who meditates while making donuts in a bakery. I read about another woman who "fills up her soul" while bicycling. And how many of us have received creative insights, spiritual or otherwise, in the shower?

We belong to a personal God, so why wouldn't some of our best soul time emerge from everyday life? If we truly believe he is omnipresent, God is just as near to us in the bathroom as in a church sanctuary or prayer closet. No matter how busy we become, we can make it our business to remain in his presence and nourish our souls.

"We can do little things for God," explained Brother Lawrence. "I turn the cake that is frying on the pan for love of Him, and that done, if there is nothing else to call me, I prostrate myself in worship before Him who has given me grace to work. Afterwards I rise happier than a king."[9]

Granted, Brother Lawrence was a monk and his peers considered lying prostrate on the floor an acceptable practice in their workplace. But even when our heads can't bow, our spirits can. While our bodies move about, our hearts can hide in God. And soon the "little things we do for God" will add up to big benefits for the soul.

Andrew Murray described this hiding of the heart as "waiting continually on the Lord." He explained that "waiting continually is a possibility. Many think that with the duties of life it is out of the question. They cannot always be thinking of it. Even when they wish to, they forget.

"They do not understand that it is a matter of the heart, and that what the heart is full of, occupies it, even when the thoughts are otherwise engaged. A father's heart may be filled continuously with intense love and longing for a sick wife or child at a distance, even though pressing business requires all his thoughts. In the midst of occupations and temptations [the heart] can wait continually."[10]

I want to find moments of inner retreat with you, Lord, but right now that seems so impossible. Plant the desire within me to wait on you continually. Show me how I can turn my heart toward you in small ways throughout the day.

PART TWO

RESTING

Leaning on Everlasting Arms

What a fellowship, what a joy divine,
Leaning on the everlasting arms;
What a blessedness, what a peace is mine,
Leaning on the everlasting arms.

Oh, how sweet to walk in this pilgrim way,
Leaning on the everlasting arms;
I have blessed peace with my Lord so near,
Leaning on the everlasting arms.

What have I to dread, what have I to fear,
Leaning on the everlasting arms;
I have blessed peace with my Lord so near,
Leaning on the everlasting arms.

Leaning, leaning,
Safe and secure from all alarms;
Leaning, leaning,
Leaning on the everlasting arms.

"Leaning on the Everlasting Arms"
by the Reverend E. A. Hoffman and A. J. Showalter

I remember when it first dawned on me that I didn't know how to relax. I'd rented a room in Aspen to attend the town's summer music festival, and a few days into this vacation, my friend JoAnne joined me for the weekend.

It soon became apparent that JoAnne and I lived by different codes. She could spend hours sitting in sidewalk cafes, sipping cold beverages, hiding behind sunglasses, and watching vacationers stroll by. I needed to go places, do things, make "good use" of my time. I shopped, attended concerts, devised sightseeing adventures, and shopped again.

As anyone could guess, JoAnne and I never truly "connected" during our time in the mountains, and we frustrated each other. After she left I replayed our differences. For JoAnne, a "holiday" was an inalienable right claimed several times a year when she cast off the world and did next to nothing. For me, a vacation occurred about once a decade when I transported my busyness to a more exotic location.

Obviously, JoAnne's definition was closer to the truth than mine. And when I dug far enough within, I quietly admitted I envied her ability to plop and do nothing. My friend's Latin and Canadian roots blessed her with a talent my German and Midwestern work ethic couldn't fathom: the ability to rest. Consequently, it took several more years and major burnout for me to ponder the meaning and necessity of rest.

The dictionary calls rest a "refreshing ease or inactivity after work or exertion,"[1] emphasizing its physical attributes. This physical cessation of activity is crucial to replenish the body and keep it healthy, but true rest delves deeper than the skin or internal organs. There is also a spiritual rest, which revives our mystical parts and reconnects us to the Creator.

To secure this soul-reviving rest, an old hymn admonishes us to lean on the everlasting arms. As a child falls back confidently in her mother's lap, so we can cradle in the heavenly Father's arms, feeling his holy breath upon us, his heartbeat next to ours.

"Come to me, all you who are weary and burdened," he beckons, "and I will give you rest."

EMPTYING THE BRAIN

On Loosening Up the Ties That Bind

The LORD is my shepherd, I shall not be in want.
He makes me lie down in green pastures,
he leads me beside quiet waters,
he restores my soul. . . .
Be at rest once more, O my soul,
for the LORD has been good to you.

—Psalm 23:1–3; 116:7

The Day-Timer catalog arrived in my home office today. Actually, the company sent me two copies, as if they know I need extra help staying organized. As I flip through the pages, this catalog assures me that if I purchase the right products, my middle-aged brain will remember everything I'm supposed to do, when I'm supposed to do it.

That's quite a promise, because I'm famous for showing up late for breakfast appointments or attending the right meeting on the wrong day. To the amusement of my former staff, I sometimes forgot what I told them to accomplish. And almost every year I ask my best friend, "Now what's the date of your birthday?" (I know the month; I just can't keep the exact day in mind.) If I make a grocery list, it rarely accompanies me to the store, and after living in this house for five years, I still struggle to remember my neighbors' names.

Due to Empty-Brain Syndrome, I fill my life with repeated reminders. In the office, I keep a daybook, a clipboard with my writing and interview schedules, a computerized calendar, piles of paper scribbled with phone messages, and yellow Post-It notes plastered in conspicuous places. I also frequently save my E-mail, voice mail, and regular mail messages for when I forget important details.

With all this forgetfulness, it's surprising that when I *want* to empty my brain for soul time, I can't. When I stop to rest or pray, the details of my to-do list march across my mental viewfinder. I ask the Lord to lead me by still waters but insist on carrying work with me and creating a paper trail in case he doesn't know the way back.

The Lord observes that I'm lugging a load of distractions, and he patiently endures them for a while. But then he gently challenges me.

"What is that in your hands?" he asks.

"Oh, just some important stuff," I reply. "Things I can't forget."

"Why don't you give them to me?" he suggests. "Then you can sit by the water and rest."

"These? Well, they're pretty crucial . . ."

He smiles and says, "Hand them over to me."

"Okay, here are the notes about my projects for work."

"But that's not all, is it? Hand everything to me. I'll watch over them."

"Everything?" I protest, but I know he's right. I'll ruin our time together if I'm distracted, and I won't be able to rest. "All right, here's the list about my family. Here are my concerns about money," I continue, and one by one I hand everything over.

"Now you can rest," he announces, smiling again.

I smile back and say, "Yes, I feel better already," and dip my feet into the water.

If we want to rest—to rest in a way that refreshes the soul—we need to loosen the ties that bind us and set them aside for a while.

How comforting to know we can hand everything—even our calendars and Post-It notes—over to God!

"Trust in the LORD and do good," wrote David. "Dwell in the land and enjoy safe pasture. Delight yourself in the LORD," and after you rest, "he will give you the desires of your heart."

Great Shepherd, I empty myself of responsibilities so I can slow down. I hand you my thoughts about work, health, family, money, friendships, and everything else that would distract me from your still waters. Fill my soul with your peace so I can rest.

UNTROUBLING THE SOUL

On Pouring Out the Desperation

My eyes are ever on the LORD,
  for only he will release my feet from the snare.
Turn to me and be gracious to me,
  for I am lonely and afflicted.
The troubles of my heart have multiplied;
  free me from my anguish.
Look upon my affliction and my distress
  and take away all my sins. . . .
Let me not be put to shame,
  for I take refuge in you.

—Psalm 25:15–18, 20

To reach a place of soul rest—to sit by still waters and lie down in green pastures—it might not be enough to hand our to-do lists to God. We may first need to pour out the desperation in our hearts, letting him know what disturbs us.

We're in pain. We feel frustrated. We don't know which way to turn. We thought life would serve us something better than this. We need to ask, "Lord, do you still remember what matters to me?" And God listens.

Before he could rest in God's goodness, the prophet Habakkuk poured out his complaints to the Creator. He asked, "How long, O

LORD, must I call for help, but you do not listen? Or cry out to you, 'Violence!' but you do not save? Why do you make me look at injustice? Why do you tolerate wrong?"

Habakkuk didn't mince words with God, and God didn't reprimand him for the outburst. Rather, he gave Habakkuk the gift of perspective. "Look at the nations and watch," said the Lord, "and be utterly amazed. For I am going to do something in your days that you would not believe, even if you were told."

After this explanation, Habakkuk dialogued with God about the prophet's agonies versus the Lord's long-range plans. When they finished, Habakkuk renewed his trust in God's ways and composed poetic, heart-stirring words of faith, in Habakkuk 3:17–19:

> Though the fig tree does not bud
>   and there are no grapes on the vines,
> though the olive crop fails
>   and the fields produce no food,
> though there are no sheep in the pen
>   and no cattle in the stalls,
> yet I will rejoice in the LORD,
>   I will be joyful in God my Savior.
> The Sovereign LORD is my strength;
>   he makes my feet like the feet of a deer,
>   he enables me to go on the heights.

Despite *not* receiving everything he wanted or not completely understanding the future, Habakkuk still rested in God's faithfulness. This is how God calls us to rest in him, too. He welcomes our honest confessions, our doubts and questions, but if we won't rest until troubles cease, we will never rest at all.

Jesus, I pour out my troubles to you. Thank you for listening to me and responding with love and understanding. Now I can rest.

GETTING TO PEACE
Offering Up the Desire to Control

Great peace have they who love your law,
    and nothing can make them stumble.
I wait for your salvation, O LORD,
    and I follow your commands.
I obey your statutes,
    for I love them greatly.
I obey your precepts and your statutes,
    for all my ways are known to you.

—Psalm 119:165–168

A T-shirt hanging in the window of a nearby resort shop exclaims, "Because I'm the MOTHER, that's why!" I laugh at the shirt's slogan and consider buying it for my sister.

I appreciate humor as a human survival skill, but despite my initial response, I realize that the T-shirt thinly masks a serious truth. We women sometimes confuse our natural responsibilities with a desire to control people and things.

In our families we're often the nurturers and detail keepers, making sure everybody gets their needs met and feels loved. These are honorable and necessary tasks, but if we're not watchful and prayerful, our strengths can easily slide into weaknesses. Being responsible turns into being controlling, and to others our acts of servanthood can feel stifling and overbearing.

Of course, we can disguise our need to control with altruistic explanations. How many of us have said these words?

"I'm only interested in your good."
"I just don't want you to get hurt."
"You don't know people like I do."
"What would *God* want you to do?"
"Don't you care about how I feel?"

When we fuel a desire to control, we're searching for peace in the wrong place. We think, *If I could just get everyone and everything in shape, then I would feel good. I could be at peace.* Actually, the opposite is true. When we give up control to God, only then do we experience inner peace and rest.

This is the core message of the Bible, and when a control binge hits, immersing in scriptural truths about the Creator's sovereignty can help us break the habit. Consider the following verses: "For the LORD most high is terrible; he is a great King over all the earth. He shall subdue the people under us, and the nations under our feet. He shall choose our inheritance for us, the excellency of Jacob whom he loved. . . . God reigneth over the heathen: God sitteth upon the throne of his holiness. The princes of the people are gathered together, even the people of the God of Abraham: for the shields of the earth belong unto God: he is greatly exalted" (Psalm 47:2–4, 8–9 KJV).

When we compare our efforts to control with God's almighty power, our endeavors look puny and silly. Still, the choice is ours. We can choose to compete with his terrible kingship and continually lose, or we can abandon control, follow his Word, and luxuriate in peace and rest.

I think the choice is obvious.

Oh, Creator, I offer up my need to control. It frustrates the people in my life, violates your sovereignty, and keeps me from resting. Help me to discern between healthy responsibility and harmful control. To remind me of my place in the world, draw me into your Word.

SLEEPING

The Forgotten Aid to Spirituality

But you are a shield around me, O LORD;
you bestow glory on me and lift up my head.
To the LORD I cry aloud,
and he answers me from his holy hill.
I lie down and sleep;
I wake again, because the LORD sustains me. . . .
Know that the LORD has set apart the godly for
himself;
the LORD will hear when I call to him. . . .
When you are on your beds,
search your hearts and be silent.

—Psalm 3:3–5; 4:3–4

According to the experts, Americans aren't getting enough sleep. In fact, these slumber statisticians say that "sleep debt" is a national crisis.

If sleep loss accumulates from night to night, sleep debt occurs, and it's impossible to recover the hours lost from this deprivation. The National Commission on Sleep Disorders reports that adults are getting twenty percent less sleep than one hundred years ago. No wonder we're so crabby.

Sleep deprivation undermines our health, blackens our mind, clouds our judgment, triggers irritability, sabotages productivity, and increases the risk of accidents. Conversely, enough sleep renders us mentally sharper, makes us able to concentrate, and helps us approach life more positively.

When we enter a deep sleep, remarkable body functions are set in motion:

- Sleep repairs tissues, reenergizes organs and muscles, and replaces old cells with new ones.
- It slows down our heartbeat, respiration, and metabolism so we obtain the needed relief from physical activity.
- This deep rest triggers the growth hormone to renew tissues, form new red blood cells, and promote bone formation.
- Sleep is also the mind's outlet for dreaming, which is essential for a healthy lifestyle.[2]

As a young woman, I dumped my anxieties on an older friend, who replied, "Sometimes the most spiritual thing we can do is get enough sleep." She knew me well, and her comment, though perplexing at that moment, proved true. When I'm pressed for time, I tend to stay up late—or sometimes all night—to accomplish tasks rather than go to bed on time and pare back activities or improve my time management skills.

However, this habit exacts a physical and spiritual toll, so I've devised these "soulish" reasons for crawling into bed:

- Sleep refurbishes my soul (mind, will, emotions) so I can respond to the world from a spiritual viewpoint.
- It makes me more positive about believing and trusting God and building my faith.
- This rest promotes physical well-being so my body's condition doesn't interfere with my soul's health and its pursuits.
- Adequate sleep keeps me alert to God's voice within and to his speaking through people and circumstances.

All told, physical rest assists our ability to walk in the Lord's way and obey his commands. Scripture says that the lessons of our spiritual fathers and mothers protect us while we sleep and speak to us when we wake up. Personally, I want to be alert enough to hear what they say to me.

Lord, I need more rest! Teach me the meaning of a child's simple prayer: "Now I lay me down to sleep, I pray the Lord my soul to keep." Please grant me deep and adequate sleep so I can alertly live from my soul.

BE STILL AND KNOW

Admitting to Our Defeat

There is a river whose streams make glad
the city of God,
the holy place where the Most High
dwells.
God is within her, she will not fall;
God will help her at break of day.
"Be still, and know that I am God;
I will be exalted among the nations,
I will be exalted in the earth."

—Psalm 46:4–5, 10

After we've struggled to set aside duties, after we've poured out the desperation, after we've given up control of the people and things around us, after we've slept off the barriers to soulish pursuits, God requires one more relinquishment before we can deeply and assuredly rest.

He says, "Be still, and know that I am God," and with this assertion he asks that we recognize his omnipotent power, his command of the universe and everything in it. Ultimately, he rules the duties, desperations, and people in our lives; he holds body and soul together while we sleep; he keeps spinning the world on its axis. Bending our knees to God's control leads us to experience an unshakable inner rest, embedded in an immutable Father's heart.

Frederick Buechner calls this submission "the magnificent defeat of the human soul at the hands of God." In his book *The Magnificent Defeat,* Buechner exemplifies this act through Jacob's all-night wrestling match with a mystical stranger by the river Jabbok.

"Out of the deep of the night a stranger leaps. He hurls himself at Jacob, and they fall to the ground, their bodies lashing through the darkness. It is terrible enough not to see the attacker's face, and his strength is more terrible still, the strength of more than a man. All the night through they struggle in silence until just before morning when it looks as though a miracle might happen. Jacob is winning. The stranger cries out to be set free before the sun rises. Then, suddenly, all is reversed.

"He merely touches the hollow of Jacob's thigh, and in a moment Jacob is lying there crippled and helpless. The sense we have, which Jacob must have had, that the whole battle was from the beginning fated to end this way, that the stranger had simply held back until now, letting Jacob exert all his strength and almost win so that when he was defeated, he would know that he was truly defeated; so that he would know that not all the shrewdness, will, brute force that he could muster were enough to get this. Jacob will not release his grip, only now it is not of violence but of need, like the grip of a drowning man.

"The darkness has faded just enough so that for the first time he can dimly see his opponent's face. And what he sees is something more terrible than the face of death—the face of love. It is vast and strong, half ruined with suffering and fierce with joy, the face a man flees down all the darkness of his days until at last he cries out, 'I will not let you go until you bless me!' Not a blessing that he can have now by the strength of his cunning or the force of his will, but a blessing that he can have only as a gift.

"Power, success, happiness, as the world knows them, are his who will fight for them hard enough; but peace, love, joy, are only from God. And God is the enemy whom Jacob fought there by the river, of course, and whom in one way or another we all of us fight—God, the beloved enemy. Our enemy because, before giving us everything, before giving us life, he demands our lives—our selves, our wills, our treasure.

"Will we give them, you and I?"[3]

Hopefully, we will reply, "Yes!"

Almighty God, I submit to your power and control. I give you everything, what I treasure most. I understand that a magnificent defeat is the only way to your blessing. I will rest in your love and care for my soul.

PART THREE

CLEANSING

Restoring the Inner Person

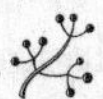

Oh, now I see the cleansing wave!
The fountain deep and wide;
Jesus, my Lord, mighty to save,
Points to His wounded side.

I rise to walk in heav'n's own light,
Above the world of sin,
With heart made pure and garments white,
And Christ enthroned within.

Amazing grace 'tis heav'n below
To feel the blood applied;
And Jesus, only Jesus, know,
My Jesus crucified.

The cleansing stream, I see, I see,
I plunge, and oh, it cleanseth me!
Oh, praise the Lord! It cleanseth me!
It cleanseth me—yes, cleanseth me.

"Cleansing Wave"

by Mrs. Phoebe Palmer and Mrs. J. F. Knapp

An ancient Celtic prayer, passed orally through the generations, expresses a believer's desire to walk so closely and openly with God that nothing lodges between them:

Be the eye of God betwixt me and each eye,
the purpose of God betwixt me and each purpose,
the hand of God betwixt me and each hand,
the shield of God betwixt me and each shield,
the desire of God betwixt me and each desire,
the bridle of God betwixt me and each bridle,
and no mouth can curse me.[1]

This verse presents a beautiful and holy request, but few of us obtain such intimacy with God. Not because it's unavailable but because through neglect we allow sin, stress, and other human-made barriers to block communication with him.

Thankfully, we can confess these obstructions to God, washing them away in the many waters of his forgiveness. Yet often we dump an unspecified load of "mistakes" at Christ's feet, asking him for a general absolution rather than naming and confessing our sins one by one. Then we wonder why our spirituality dulls, why our souls muddle up with more sin.

This one-by-one naming isn't meant to punish us but to acknowledge our debt and later remind us, when doubt strikes, that we're irrevocably forgiven. We can remember confessing the sin; we can rely on God's promise that he cleansed us; we can stop replaying a grievance in our mind. We can know there is nothing between God and us.

We can sing, "Nothing between my soul and the Savior, So that His blessed face may be seen; Nothing preventing the least of His favor, Keep the way clear! Let nothing between."[2]

There is "nothing between" because we are cleansed. The soul is unencumbered and free.

SAYING THE SIN
Repenting and Erasing Guilt

Have mercy on me, O God,
according to your unfailing love;
according to your great compassion
blot out my transgressions.
Wash away all my iniquity
and cleanse me from my sin.
For I know my transgressions,
and my sin is always before me. . . .
Cleanse me with hyssop, and I will be clean;
wash me, and I will be whiter than snow.

—Psalm 51:1–3, 7

On a sunny day in Chicago, a solemn-looking man stood stiffly on a busy downtown street corner. As people hurried past, he'd slowly lift his arm, point to an unsuspecting pedestrian, and yell, "Guilty!"

Without expression the man would return to his stiff stance for a while. Then he'd raise his arm again and scream, "Guilty!" at another startled person.

The atmosphere turned eerie. Each time the man yelled his judgment, people stared at him, hesitated, and looked away. Or they looked at each other and then hurried down the sidewalk as if they'd been exposed. One passerby even turned to a stranger and asked, "How did *he* know?"[3]

Guilt. It's an old, familiar feeling. So familiar that for many of us it's a way of life. We can't push beyond our guilt to God's love and forgiveness, and this inactivity stunts our emotional and spiritual growth.

Much of our inability to experience true forgiveness originates when we feel sorry for our mistakes instead of repentant for our sin. Sorriness only bobs on the surface of wrongdoing; repentance dives to the bottom of sin and eradicates it. Saying "I'm sorry" just admits getting caught; it doesn't force us to topple pride and view the spiritual wreckage. Naming the specific offense and saying "I repent" acknowledges our sin and expresses a desire to turn from it. Sorriness evokes emotion. Repentance, though often tearful, willfully decides to change.

We can express repentance with a method that's meaningful to us: alone or with a trusted friend; in our words or through liturgy; in our heart or with our lips. It's the end result that matters: a clear-cut confession of our iniquity before God and the humble request that he forgive us. At certain times we may need to confess offenses accumulated over the years: those we've never admitted; those we've recently recognized as sin; those we've confessed but keep repeating. This could require extended prayer and confession but often reaps spiritual renewal.

While serving as a pastor, Richard Foster desired more power in his spiritual walk. So he devised a plan of thorough repentance by dividing his life into three periods: childhood, adolescence, adulthood. After a prayer for God's guidance, he wrote down anything from these periods that needed forgiveness or healing or both.

Paper in hand, Richard then met with a Christian friend and read the list aloud. When he finished reading, Richard began to place the list in a briefcase, but his friend intercepted the paper, shredded it to bits, and dropped the pieces into a wastebasket. He then prayed for the healing of the hurts in Richard's past.

And Richard knew, with absolute certainty, that God forgave him.[4]

Savior, one at a time I name my sins to you. I accept your forgiveness and put these transgressions behind me. Remind me to daily confess my sins, not fearing your punishment but looking forward to your grace.

JOURNEY TO FORGIVENESS

Giving Eternal Grace to Others

Create in me a pure heart, O God,
    and renew a steadfast spirit within me.
Do not cast me from your presence
    or take your Holy Spirit from me.
Restore to me the joy of your salvation
    and grant me a willing spirit, to sustain me.
Then I will teach transgressors your ways,
    and sinners will turn back to you.

—Psalm 51:10–13

There are times when repentance doesn't immediately usher us into cleansing streams. Quite often we must grant forgiveness before accepting it. The Lord Jesus taught us to pray, "Forgive us our debts, as we also have forgiven our debtors." Getting and granting forgiveness is a hand-in-glove arrangement.

So if others have wronged us, we need to forgive them—sometimes face-to-face, other times just before God. As with repentance, this step requires a willful decision more than an emotional upheaval. It varies with circumstances and personalities.

After two thousand years Jesus Christ's advice to forgive those who hurt us still reaps results. He knew that in addition to blocking the mind, ravaging the emotions, and hurting our health, unforgiveness stunts spiritual growth and a relationship with God. And in a mysterious way, it stops the movement of forgiveness toward us.

Jesus' conversation with Peter, recorded in Matthew 18, elaborates on this spiritual principle. "How many times do I have to forgive somebody who hurts me?" asked Peter. "Maybe seven times?" "No," Jesus replied. "It's seventy times seven."

Then Jesus told a parable about an unforgiving servant, comparing the story to the spiritual kingdom. When a king decided to settle his financial accounts, the ruler discovered a servant who could not pay back the considerable money he owed. "Sell all of his belongings, including his wife and children, to settle this servant's debt," commanded the king.

The terrified servant fell to his knees and begged, "Please, sir, have mercy on me! Give me more time, and I will pay back all that I owe." The king felt compassion, forgave the servant's debt, and freed him.

Then the servant visited a friend who owed him money and insisted it be repaid immediately. "Have mercy," pleaded the friend, but the servant refused. Instead he asked the authorities to throw the friend into prison until he paid the debt.

When the king heard about the servant's unforgiveness, he asked him, "Shouldn't you express the same kind of forgiveness that I showed to you?" Then the king ordered the hypocritical man slammed into prison and tortured until he paid the original debt.

With a memorable punch line Jesus concluded, "This is how God will treat you if you do not forgive one another from the heart."

The Great Teacher delivered a startling message to underscore the spiritual importance of praying, "Forgive us our debts, as we forgive our debtors." When we don't forgive, we won't be forgiven. Our spiritual selves deteriorate.

The world peacemaker Dag Hammarskjöld described forgiveness as "the answer to the child's dream of a miracle by which what is broken is made whole again, what is soiled is again made clean."[5]

We think of this mending and cleansing as a gift to our offender, and it can be. It releases that person from the guilt, negativity, and complications of a battered relationship. But forgiveness also extends grace to ourselves. It heals what's destroying us inside.

Forgiving Lord, I harbor resentment and bitterness toward someone. Work in me so I'm willing to forgive this person from the heart. I want to be free from the bitterness destroying me inside. Instead of being a prisoner to this person's offense, I want to release him (or her) to your care.

GRABBING GRACE

Forgiving Ourselves for Failing

Blessed is he
    whose transgressions are forgiven,
    whose sins are covered.
Blessed is the man
    whose sin the LORD does not count
        against him
    and in whose spirit is no deceit. . . .
I acknowledged my sin to you
    and did not cover up my iniquity.
I said, "I will confess
    my transgressions to the LORD"—
and you forgave
    the guilt of my sin.

—Psalm 32:1–2, 5

Once we've pardoned others, forgiveness doesn't finish there. It's equally important to forgive ourselves. This is probably the hardest step, especially for women. We often find it difficult to forgive ourselves. We repeatedly flog ourselves to prove true repentance, when in reality we're exposing our inability to grab God's grace.

The apostle Peter exhibited self-forgiveness. He "went outside and wept bitterly" after denying Jesus Christ three times to protect himself. Then when Jesus forgave him and said, "Feed my lambs," Peter rallied and became a great spiritual leader.

At some point Peter must have forgiven himself. He believed and fulfilled the prophecy that he'd become the rock on which Christ would build the church. After Christ's ascension, the former disciple performed miracles and stood stalwart through persecution. But he couldn't have wielded such spiritual power while wallowing in unforgiveness.

Self-forgiveness needs exercise in many areas. It's necessary for absolving everyday mistakes, such as disobeying the boss, yelling at the kids, or gossiping with a friend. It's also required for life-changing failures—ignoring God's call, marrying the wrong man, or choosing a sinful lifestyle. If we truly repent, God will forgive any sin we've committed. So why shouldn't we forgive ourselves? Why shouldn't our souls be free?

Mother Angelica, a nun who manages a Christian television network, teaches a simple truth about self-forgiveness. One day while standing by the sea, a wave splashed her, and she sensed the Lord asking, "Angelica, do you see the drop on your finger?"

"Yes."

"It represents your sin. Do you also see the vast ocean?"

"Yes, I see that too, Lord."

"The ocean represents my mercy. If you fling the droplet into the sea, could you find it again?"

"No."

"The same is true for your droplet of sin and my ocean of mercy. You can keep your offenses and stay miserable or you can lose them in my mercy. What will you do?"

Angelica flung the droplet into the sea.[6]

So can we.

Merciful Father, following Peter's example I forgive myself for my sins. Though my tendency is to relive the offenses and keep flogging myself, I choose to cast them into your waters of forgiveness. Thank you for cleansing me.

TOUCH THE WOUND

Healing What Hinders the Soul's Growth

The LORD builds up Jerusalem;
he gathers the exiles of Israel.
He heals the brokenhearted
and binds up their wounds. . . .
Great is our Lord and mighty in power;
his understanding has no limit.
The LORD sustains the humble
but casts the wicked to the ground.

—Psalm 147:2–3, 5–6

In her book *Composing a Life,* Mary Catherine Bateson described her years as dean of the faculty at Amherst College. During that time, Mary observed the subversion of female faculty members.

She explained, "The subversion was accomplished by taking advantage of two kinds of vulnerability that women raised in our society tend to have. The first is the quality of self-sacrifice, a learned willingness to set their own interests aside and be used and even used up by the community. . . .

"The second kind of vulnerability trained into women is a readiness to believe messages of disdain and derogation. Even women who arrived at Amherst full of confidence gradually became vulnerable to distorted visions of themselves, no longer secure that their sense of who they were matched the perceptions of others. And all of this is available as a bad model for the next generation."[7]

These vulnerabilities permeate the hearts of many women today, as evidenced by our low self-esteem. Derogatory messages that contribute to a poor self-image can begin within the family circle, but even with a loving, supportive home life, women emerge into a world that repeatedly devalues their worth.

As the daughter of anthropologist Margaret Mead, Mary lived with an example of a woman's valuable, unconventional contribution to society. Yet Mary openly admitted, "I have slighted my own value so often that it is hard to learn to take it seriously. Instead, I get things done by finding rationales for the task and then sacrificing myself for it."[8]

Needless to say, devaluing ourselves wounds the soul. Instinctively, the soul knows it was "fearfully and wonderfully" created in God's image. Yet repeated onslaughts against this truth damage our ability to live fully for his kingdom, accomplishing its sacred work in the world. Unfortunately, we can grow so accustomed to living with poor self-esteem, we don't recognize it as a debilitating wound. We think we're supposed to feel this lousy about ourselves.

Just as we plunge our sins into the waters of forgiveness, we can also cleanse and heal our wounded self-esteem there. We can heal *any* wound there. The prophet Isaiah predicted Christ's suffering so we can be healed. He wrote, "Surely he took up our infirmities and carried our sorrows. . . . But he was pierced for our transgressions, he was crushed for our iniquities; the punishment that brought us peace was upon him, and by his wounds we are healed."

Because Jesus was wounded, he can cleanse and touch our wounds, and his touch heals and restores pain and brokenness. May our hearts understand this: as often as we confess our sins, we can also ask for his healing. As much as he desires to forgive our sins, he also longs to heal us.

Holy Jesus, please heal my low self-esteem and other wounds that contribute to it. Wash my wounds in your cleansing waters, then touch and restore me for your service.

PART FOUR

SURRENDERING

Giving All to a Generous God

Saviour, 'tis a full surrender,
All I have to follow Thee;
Thou my Leader and Defender
From this hour shalt ever be!

As I come in deep contrition,
At this consecrated hour,
Hear, O Christ, my heart's petition,
Let me feel the Spirit's power!

Oh, the joy of full salvation!
Oh, the peace of love divine!
Oh, the bliss of consecration—
I am His, and He is mine!

I surrender all! I surrender all!
All I have I bring to Jesus,
I surrender all!

"Full Surrender"
by Rebecca S. Pollard and D. B. Towner

You'd think Joseph would have known better. Wearing his coat of many colors, reporting to his father his brothers' bad behavior, talking about dreams in which relatives bowed down to him—he almost asked for trouble. So before long, jealous and resentful family members ousted Joseph from home.

Sold by his brothers to Midianite traders, then to an officer in Pharaoh's house, Joseph entered Egypt a humbled man. Yet he decided to work diligently at the tasks assigned to him and surrendered the outcome to God. From servant to prisoner to Egyptian ruler, Joseph turned hardship into submission and service to his adopted homeland.

Years later his brothers, unaware of Joseph's identity, requested food from him because of famine in their land. Joseph obliged, eventually revealed his identity, and reunited with his family. "Don't be afraid," he told his brothers. "Am I in the place of God? You intended to harm me, but God intended it for good to accomplish what is now being done, the saving of many lives."

Whether we willingly commit or whether we bend our knees from desperation, God asks us to surrender ourselves, our plans and desires, to him. First, because he is the Lord of everything and deserves our submission. Second, because his plans loom greater and more fulfilling than ours. Jesus taught, "Seek first his kingdom and his righteousness, and all these things will be given to you as well."

Often "all these things" exceed our expectations and sometimes extend beyond our earthly lives.

"Why are you here?" the Indian women asked missionary Amy Carmichael. "Where are your relatives? Why have you left them and come here? What does the government give you for coming here?" During her first years in India, Amy probably asked herself the same questions, but she surrendered to God's call and stayed.

Not long after, she learned about the appalling practice of committing young girls to temple prostitution. Soon Amy devoted her energies to saving them. Taking in temple runaways, she established the Dohnavur Fellowship, which grew to include nurseries, bedrooms, a hospital, classrooms, workrooms, gardens, farms and pastures, hostels, playing fields, and other resources for nine hundred residents.

The Dohnavur Fellowship still thrives today, decades after her death. So do Amy's books and letters to friends and Fellowship workers. When she surrendered to a generous God, he gave back to Amy in ways she never imagined.

He can do the same for us.

FORSAKING THE WORLD

The Meaning of Being Separate

Blessed is the man
  who does not walk in the counsel of
    the wicked
or stand in the way of sinners
  or sit in the seat of mockers.
But his delight is in the law of the LORD,
  and on his law he meditates day and night.
He is like a tree planted by streams of water,
  which yields its fruit in season
and whose leaf does not wither.
Whatever he does prospers.

—Psalm 1:1–3

Before his conversion to Christianity, Saint Augustine lived raucously. From the example of his mother, Augustine knew what a life "separated unto God" looked like, but he couldn't paint that picture for himself.

In his book *Confessions,* Augustine recounted the sins of his youth and how his prayers rang with insincerity. "Give me chastity and continence," he told God, "but not yet."[1] Augustine eventually changed his prayer, and through his writings we can learn about dedicating ourselves wholly to God.

We can identify with Augustine's earlier indecision, though. If we're to keep growing from the soul, we reach a turning point when God asks us to stop waffling and wholeheartedly commit to him. As a result of our spiritual cleansing and healing, he calls us to "come out from them and be separate," forsaking the unclean.

Satan, the enemy of our souls, would have us believe that this calling will sap us of pleasure and contentment, but this lie doesn't deter God, nor can it stop us from responding.

The Lord asks, "Are you willing to follow only me? Will you let me captivate your soul more tightly and penetrate it more deeply? Will you allow me to wash away what still clings inside you? Will you discover joy and purity in me?" His voice sounds so compelling, his love feels so enveloping, we can't help but follow him despite our fears. But when we answer yes, it suddenly looks as though our fears and the Devil's warnings will prove true, because Jesus leads us down a narrow and hazardous path.

"The way is unutterably hard, and every moment we are in danger of straying from it," admitted the Christian martyr Dietrich Bonhoeffer. "If we follow this way as one we follow in obedience to an external command, if we are afraid of ourselves all the time, it is indeed an impossible way. But if we behold Jesus Christ going on before us step by step, we shall not go astray. If we worry about the dangers that beset us, if we gaze at the road instead of at him who goes before, we are already straying from the path. For he is himself the way, the narrow way and the strait gate. He, and he alone, is our journey's end.

"When we know that, we are able to proceed along the narrow way through the strait gate of the cross, and on to eternal life, and the very narrowness of the road will increase our certainty. The way which the Son of God trod on earth, and the way which we too must tread as citizens of two worlds on the razor edge between this world and the kingdom of heaven could hardly be a broad way. The narrow way is bound to be right."[2]

Will we choose the right way? Each of us must answer individually. But when we think of this way, we can remember that it is a *relationship* more than a journey, an invitation to walk alone with a lover more than a narrowing footpath. And suddenly, being "separate" sounds intimate rather than stifling or frightening.

Christ Jesus, I long to be separated and set apart for you, but it sounds too hard. Gently teach me that if I follow the narrow path out of love for you, it will be a fulfilling journey.

DARING TO GO DEEPER

In Search of Something More

The LORD has dealt with me according to my
righteousness;
according to the cleanness of my hands he has
rewarded me.
For I have kept the ways of the LORD;
I have not done evil by turning from my
God. . . .
To the faithful you show yourself faithful,
to the blameless you show yourself blameless,
to the pure you show yourself pure.

—Psalm 18:20–21, 25–26

Years ago I worshiped at a church whose pastor, in his early days of ministry, apprenticed under A. W. Tozer, a man called a twentieth-century prophet. For several decades until his death in the 1960s, Tozer rattled conservative Christianity by insisting that the church as a whole, as well as its individual members, needed a fuller spiritual experience.

This "deeper life" claimed all of the power, holiness, and blessing the Holy Spirit intended for believers. Some called this experience the "victorious life," but Tozer considered the term a misnomer because it emphasized only one aspect of a Christian's walk with God. He wrote that the deeper life "is far wider and richer than mere victory over sin, however vital that victory might be." It also includes the "thought of the indwelling Christ, acute God-consciousness, rapturous worship, separation from the world, the joyous surrender of everything to God, internal union with the Trinity, the practice of God's presence, the communion of saints and prayer without ceasing."

Influenced by Tozer's teachings and his own journey with the Holy Spirit, my pastor repeatedly exhorted us to "lay down our lives." Like his mentor, he believed the deeper life emerged with great cost: a full surrender to God.

"To enter upon such a life," wrote Tozer, "seekers must be ready to accept without question the New Testament as the one final authority on spiritual matters. They must be willing to make Christ the one supreme Lord and ruler in their lives. They must surrender their whole being to the destructive power of the cross, to die not only to their sins but to their righteousness as well as to everything in which they formerly prided themselves."

As I listened to my pastor, read a few of Tozer's books, and pondered this straightforward message about surrender, I shuddered. This sounded much too costly and invasive, as if when God filled my soul, I'd be left a meaningless blob. Mistakenly I emphasized the first half of the deeper-life equation (full surrender) and ignored the rewarding second half (absolute joy). I didn't consider that what I'd lose (my sinful, selfish ways) would be replaced with something far better and sweeter (the Holy Spirit's attributes within me).

Perhaps many Christians struggle with this misconception, because Tozer added, "The mighty anointing of the Holy Spirit that follows will restore to the soul infinitely more than what has been taken away. Those who have known the sweetness of it will never complain about what they have lost. They will be too well pleased with what they have gained."[3]

When considering a full surrender to God, we can fear what we'll lose instead of taking heart in what we'll gain. Realistically, though, life-changing decisions—even the joyful choices—require giving up one thing to gain another, losing a part of ourselves to find a different and better part. (Think about the decisions to marry, have children, gain employment, or pursue healing.)

Jesus said that if we clutch our lives, we'll lose them, but if we abandon our lives, we'll regain them. As always, the choice is ours. But it doesn't take the wisdom of Solomon to discern that it's far better to surrender and reap everlasting spiritual rewards than to fight for what's temporal and lose everything, even our souls, in the end.

Lord, I want a deeper spiritual life than I possess now, but my sinful soul fights against it. Help me! Lead me to a place of full surrender to you. Help me not to fear what I will lose, because I'll be gaining more of you.

LOSING YOUR LIFE

Throwing Away Self-Made Plans

Into your hands I commit my spirit;
    redeem me, O LORD, the God of truth. . . .
My times are in your hands;
    deliver me from my enemies
    and from those who pursue me.
Let your face shine on your servant;
    save me in your unfailing love. . . .
How great is your goodness,
    which you have stored up for those who
      fear you,
which you bestow in the sight of men
    on those who take refuge in you.

—Psalm 31:5, 15–16, 19

Today is my birthday. With its arrival I realize that many of my best-laid plans and deepest desires for life haven't materialized. Or at best they've crashed and burned.

I'm not married, nor do I have children. I don't own the house I live in and cherish. I don't travel the globe. I don't earn a six-figure income. The biggest passion of my life—a magazine launch I dreamed and prayed about for ten years, then worked on for five more years—died after publishing four issues. As a result, I lost my job and became self-employed—two items high on my list of "Things I Never Want to Do." To top it off, business is slow now, and I'm not certain how I'll pay the rent.

From all appearances I should be a disgruntled and disillusioned woman. Instead, my soul's delight is steadily increasing. Not because I've attained a saintly and disciplined spirituality but because I've stumbled onto an ancient soulish principle: If we give up our desires and accept God's plans, we gain a peace that passes understanding. I used to think this peace descended only when we *voluntarily* surrendered our plans. Not so. The desires I listed earlier were withheld or wrested from me. The key has been cooperation.

When we suffer loss, when God delays our requests, we can fight and grow bitter, or cooperate by leaning into the pain and grabbing his hand. We can say, "I don't understand, but I accept that you've allowed these circumstances." Or as Jesus would say, "Not my will, Father, but thine be done." Uttering these words frees the soul to fill with the Spirit, to remold in his image, to focus on what really matters.

This submission also opens us to surprise. We may discover that despite our striving and asking, God knows best about who we're created to be and what will satisfy us. In my case, since childhood I'd felt called to be an author, but as an adult I couldn't muster the courage to write full-time. "Someday I'll do it if I win a sweepstakes or have a husband to help support me," I'd explain. Besides, I wanted to accomplish other plans and projects first.

After years of my excuses, God probably had heard enough. He flung me into the freelance writing world, and I'm gathering new information about myself. For example, I like creating products without the obstacles of corporate politics. I enjoy the flexibility in my schedule. I'm relaxed working at home. I love publishing books. (Like most authors, I wrestle with writing but I love having written!) I appreciate regaining my personal life.

Essentially, I'm doing what I didn't plan to do but everything I'm destined to accomplish. I imagined being a full-time writer but not this soon, this way. God has fulfilled a dream but with enough uncertainties to necessitate daily faith and surrender. And while my bank account has emptied, my soul has fattened.

This is often God's way. He lands us in circumstances so we'll put his kingdom first; then if we consent, he lavishly fills us with himself. Wrapped in his arms we wonder, *Why didn't I surrender sooner?*

Lord, my plans and desires remain unfulfilled and I don't understand why. Though I'm hurting, I surrender them to you. Please fatten my soul with you and your plans. Fill me with your peace that passes understanding.

NOT MY WILL

Living as a Daily Sacrifice

Know that the LORD has set apart the godly for
  himself;
 the LORD will hear when I call to him. . . .
Offer right sacrifices
 and trust in the LORD. . . .
 Let the light of your face shine upon us,
  O LORD.
You have filled my heart with greater joy
 than when their grain and new wine abound.

—Psalm 4:3, 5–7

An exasperated friend once exclaimed, "I hate that life is so daily!"

I understand what she meant. In a perfect world, my life would be crammed with exotic places to visit, intriguing people to entertain, accolades for my creative work, plenty of leisure time, and enough money to finance it all.

That description isn't even close to reality.

While writing books, I'm cloistered in the house, away from friends and family, tapping on a computer keyboard and racking my brains for ideas. Readers of an author's newly released work may imagine publishing as glamorous, but for most writers it's a persistent plodding along. As my friend would say, a writer's life is "very daily." In other words, it's a continual grind with the possibility of always working in obscurity.

Life is this way for most of us. We experience highs and lows, but wedged in between are huge slices of ordinary, unacclaimed living. Sometimes we fear these times will stretch endlessly into the future, without purpose or meaning. We prefer variety and stimulation over the repetitive and mind-numbing nature of daily tasks. Just how many times can we wash the dishes, add up numbers, drive the kids to school, or work at a machine without feeling insignificant?

With God, as many times as we need to.

These mundane days and tasks, like everything else in a believer's life, can be offered to God as sweet-smelling sacrifices. We can find meaning in them because we've given our lives, our very moments, our daily responsibilities to him. The kitchen, the office, the minivan, the factory can serve as holy altars to God—places where we surrender, obey, and please him.

I love how this old poem expresses the delight of a soul accomplishing everyday tasks:

There are strange ways of serving God;
You sweep a room or turn a sod,
And suddenly, to your surprise,
You hear the whir of seraphim,
And find you're under God's own eyes
And building palaces for Him.[4]

God has ordained our days, so we delight him by plodding through the ordinary times. And amazingly, we find him in the "dailyness" with us.

Ever-present God, I offer up my daily life and tasks to you. Thank you that I can serve you even during these seemingly insignificant times. My soul surrenders and says, "Not my will but yours be done, Lord."

TASTE THE JOY

Filling Up with Holiness

I will praise the LORD, who counsels me;
even at night my heart instructs me.
I have set the LORD always before me.
Because he is at my right hand,
I will not be shaken....
You have made known to me the path of life;
you will fill me with joy in your presence,
with eternal pleasures at your right hand.

—Psalm 16:7–8, 11

Not long after graduating from college, when it was "cool" and countercultural for young Christians to meet God anywhere but a church building, I visited a worship service in a gymnasium. The Sunday morning gathering felt unremarkable except for a twentysomething man who led the singing.

He sat unpretentiously on a stool, strummed his guitar, and sang along with the group instead of controlling its musical praise. I sensed his humility, but mostly I gazed at his radiant face.

However, his countenance isn't what I remember most. Throughout each song he'd lean back his head and release a laugh like I had never heard before (or for that matter, haven't heard much since). Something in me immediately recognized it as a holy laugh, brimming with God's love and purity. A laugh full of joy and self-abandonment; a laugh so captivating, I can still hear it twenty years later.

Today I'd call this young man's sound a "laugh of surrender" because he allowed God to express himself—to laugh—through him. Some of us surrender to God more reluctantly than others, but once we fill with the Spirit's holiness, we don't forget it. I've tasted this sweetness only a few times in my spiritual life, each at a point of surrender. When I returned to God after years of spiritual rebellion and when I committed myself to a life purpose of "publishing the glad tidings," the Spirit rushed through me momentarily. I felt God's presence in my soul as never before.

The most profound experience, however, descended over a simple obedience rather than a life-changing decision. At his prompting, I told God I'd give part of my salary to a financially struggling family for as long as needed. I had barely uttered these words when a powerful sensation rose from within and spilled out my mouth. It was a holy, joyful, almost indescribable feeling. It told me this commitment pleased God.

I relate these stories not to sound pious but to encourage. If a flawed, willful, ordinary woman like me can encounter the holy, anyone can. Anyone who will obey and surrender. When the prophet Isaiah encountered God's holiness, he cried, "Woe to me! I am ruined! For I am a man of unclean lips, and I live among a people of unclean lips, and my eyes have seen the King, the LORD Almighty." Isaiah expressed what people through the ages have felt when accosted by the holy God.

Thankfully, God doesn't let us choke on our filth. As with Isaiah, he takes away our guilt and atones for our sins. The resulting joy and presence of God feels so rapturous that we can't help but surrender again and echo the prophet's words, "Here I am, Lord, send me!"

Holy God, I will step aside so you can fill me with your presence and joy. I will not fear but welcome the Spirit's expression through me, even a "laugh of surrender."

PART FIVE

SEEKING

Meeting God in Prayer

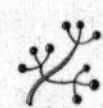

Prayer is the soul's sincere desire,
Unuttered or expressed;
The motion of a hidden fire
That trembles in the breast.

Prayer is the burden of a sigh;
The falling of a tear;
The upward glancing of an eye,
When none but God is near.

Prayer is the contrite sinner's voice
Returning from his ways,
While angels in their songs rejoice,
And say—"Behold, he prays."

Prayer is the Christian's vital breath,
The Christian's native air,
His watchword at the gate of death:
He enters heaven with prayer.

"Prayer Is the Soul's Sincere Desire"
by J. Montgomery and William H. Havergal

In the introduction to her book *Adventures in Prayer,* Catherine Marshall outlined the requirements for admission to the School of Prayer. She explained, "Admittance to the School of Prayer is by an entrance test with only two questions. The first one is: Are you in real need? The second is: Do you admit that you are helpless to handle that need?

"Whatever I learned about prayer has come as the result of times when I could answer a resounding *yes* to both questions. Looking back over my life, those times of need stand out like mountain peaks rather than, as one might suppose, valleys of despond. Peaks—because each time I learned something important about God—how real He is and how gloriously able to answer prayer.

"In childhood one of those times of learning came through my desperate fear of the dark. In my teens, there was the dire need of funds for college. At twenty-seven the need was a serious illness. The peak in my thirties was the gigantic one of my husband Peter Marshall's sudden death, along with lesser hills of need: how to rear a son without his father, how to find a career for myself at this point in life and without any specialized training.

"Years later, after my marriage to Leonard LeSourd and the taking on of three children, it was back to the School of Prayer again. As usual, there was no problem about passing the entrance test; my need was great, my inadequacy obvious.

"More often, of course, the situation that drove me to my knees was not so intensely personal. The need might be a friend's—or one I had only read about somewhere in our war-torn and hungry world. But always the criteria held: great needs and insufficient resources of my own with which to meet them.

"The halls and classrooms of the School of Prayer are crowded as never before because our needs press upon us with new urgency: worldwide economic crises, marriage problems on the rise, a widening generation gap, drug addiction, alcoholism, cancer of almost epidemic frequency. No wonder we rush to the school! Our thirst is deep, our eagerness to learn is enormous.

"What good news it is that our very inadequacy is the master key swinging wide the door to His adequacy. Forever and forever our thirst and hunger drive us to 'taste and see that the Lord is good.' Who but Jesus could ever have thought of a plan like that!"[1]

Are you ready to enter the School of Prayer?

PETITION
Asking the Father for Help

Give ear to my words, O LORD,
consider my sighing.
Listen to my cry for help,
my King and my God,
for to you I pray.
In the morning, O LORD, you hear my voice;
in the morning I lay my requests before you
and wait in expectation. . . .
I, by your great mercy,
will come into your house;
in reverence will I bow down
toward your holy temple.

—Psalm 5:1–3, 7

In my spiritual journey I've struggled with prayer, especially in regard to petitioning God with my requests. Instead of simply asking him for help, I've asked myself questions: Will God really hear? Will he care about what matters to me? Should I only ask him for big, life-changing decisions? Do I have enough faith to ask? Do I *deserve* to ask? Am I asking for too much, too often?

I've found answers in the Bible.

Instead of creating my own lists and explanations, I offer these Scriptures as the reasons we can boldly petition God with our requests:

> "Ask and it will be given to you; seek and you will find; knock and the door will be opened to you. For everyone who asks receives; he who seeks finds; and to him who knocks, the door will be opened.
>
> "Which of you, if his son asks for bread, will give him a stone? Or if he asks for a fish, will give him a snake? If you, then, though you are evil, know how to give good gifts to your children, how much more will your Father in heaven give good gifts to those who ask him!"
>
> —MATTHEW 7:7–11

> "I tell you the truth, if anyone says to this mountain, 'Go, throw yourself into the sea,' and does not doubt in his heart but believes that what he says will happen, it will be done for him. Therefore I tell you, whatever you ask for in prayer, believe that you have received it, and it will be yours."
>
> —MARK 11:23–24

> "If you remain in me and my words remain in you, ask whatever you wish, and it will be given you."
>
> —JOHN 15:7

> And pray in the Spirit on all occasions with all kinds of prayers and requests. With this in mind, be alert and always keep on praying for all the saints.
>
> —EPHESIANS 6:18

> Do not be anxious about anything, but in everything, by prayer and petition, with thanksgiving, present

your requests to God. And the peace of God, which transcends all understanding, will guard your hearts and your minds in Christ Jesus.

—PHILIPPIANS 4:6–7

If any of you lacks wisdom, he should ask God, who gives generously to all without finding fault, and it will be given to him.

—JAMES 1:5

Therefore confess your sins to each other and pray for each other so that you may be healed. The prayer of a righteous man is powerful and effective.

Elijah was a man just like us. He prayed earnestly that it would not rain, and it did not rain on the land for three and a half years. Again he prayed, and the heavens gave rain, and the earth produced its crops.

—JAMES 5:16–18

Generous God, I boldly bring my request to you. I will ask so it may be given to me. I will seek so I can find the answer and knock until the door opens to me. Please hear and answer my prayer.

INTERCESSION
Asking on Behalf of Others

Hear my prayer, O LORD;
 let my cry for help come to you.
Do not hide your face from me
 when I am in distress.
Turn your ear to me;
 when I call, answer me quickly. . . .
You will arise and have compassion on Zion,
 for it is time to show favor to her;
 the appointed time has come. . . .
For the LORD will rebuild Zion
 and appear in his glory.
He will respond to the prayer of the destitute;
 he will not despise their plea.

—Psalm 102:1–2, 13, 16–17

Since the nineteenth century, George Muller has served as a testament to the remarkable power of intercessory prayer. Due to his insatiable prayer life, Muller's orphanage for children in Bristol, England, received over "a million pounds sterling," and more than thirty thousand people decided to follow Christ. In some cases, he prayed for people's salvation for more than fifty years.

Muller credited his faith-filled prayer to five conditions. He explained, "In observing these I have the assurance of answer to my prayer:

"1. I have not the least doubt because I am assured that it is the Lord's will to save them, for He willeth that all men should be saved, and come to the knowledge of the truth. Also, we have the assurance if we ask anything according to His will, He heareth us.

"2. I have never pleaded for their salvation in my own name, but in the blessed name of my precious Lord Jesus, and on His merits alone.

"3. I always firmly believed in the willingness of God to answer my prayers.

"4. I am not conscious of having yielded to any sin, for 'if I regard iniquity in my heart, the Lord will not hear me' when I call.

"5. I have persevered in believing prayer for more than fifty-two years for some, and shall continue till the answer comes: 'Shall not God avenge his own elect, which cry day and night unto him?' "[2]

Aside from asking God to cleanse him from sin, Muller's confidence in prayer stemmed from praying God's will for others. We can always feel confident praying for someone's spiritual salvation; this is God's expressed will for all people. But in other matters, praying "according to God's will" may not be as immediately apparent.

When we intercede for people, we can confuse our desires with God's best for them. We can pray a version of "God, make them do what I want them to do!" Or we can use the request "Not my will but thine be done" to avoid the work of spiritually discerning their needs and exercising our faith. Effective intercession falls somewhere in between. We set aside our desires and ask God, "What would you have me to pray? What is your desire for them?" and pray accordingly.

"To pray . . . is to desire; but it is to desire what God would have us desire," wrote the seventeenth-century archbishop Fénelon. "He who desires not from the bottom of the heart, offers a deceitful prayer."[3] Besides interceding for other people's needs and souls, praying selflessly strengthens our souls, too. It keeps us honest before God.

"Surely you desire truth in the inner parts," sang King David. "You teach me wisdom in the inmost place." That wisdom will show us how to pray fully, purely, and unceasingly for others.

God, grant me the wisdom to know how to pray for others. I confess my sins and selfish desires; I don't want self-motivated preferences to color my intercession for these people. Lord, I ask that your will be done for them.

CONVERSATION

Taking Time to Talk with God

Come and listen, all you who fear God;
let me tell you what he has done for me.
I cried out to him with my mouth;
his praise was on my tongue.
If I had cherished sin in my heart,
the Lord would not have listened;
but God has surely listened
and heard my voice in prayer.
Praise be to God,
who has not rejected my prayer
or withheld his love from me!

—Psalm 66:16–20

During John Steinbeck's later years, his wife, Elaine, brought home a paperback biography of her husband. It was *Steinbeck* by Frank William Watt.

Steinbeck, who felt that commentators often misunderstood his life and writing, read the book with great interest. Finished, he remarked to Elaine, "This book doesn't seem to be about me, but it's pretty interesting about somebody." Obviously, the biographer hadn't spent time with Steinbeck, learning about the man behind the work.[4]

We can treat God the same way: talking about him, interpreting him, even writing about him, but not getting to know him through day-to-day conversation and companionship. The Bible encourages us to pray continually, but how can we accomplish this? We've so many activities to do and think about, how do we keep up with God, too?

God dwells with us continually, so we can consider him a companion, with us wherever we go. Conversations with a companion usually divide into two categories: maintaining and probing. In maintenance conversations we ask questions to receive quick information, comment on everyday occurrences, listen while our hands keep busy, tell funny and interesting stories, give necessary (and sometimes unnecessary) instructions, mention topics that need more discussion later, or say, "How's it going?" when we can only see each other periodically. We converse through the flow of a day, responding to events and maintaining the relationship.

Probing conversations *are* events. We stop and talk more deeply and meaningfully. We hear, listen, and respond more carefully. We wrestle with problems, explain our requests, review our days, catch up on current thinking, explore each other's desires, seek definitive answers and activities, affirm our hopes and plans. These conversations affect our well-being, self-esteem, and sense of direction. They grow a relationship and feed the soul.

Through prayer we can conduct both kinds of conversations with God. In either case, an effective conversationalist commits herself to talking and listening, hearing and responding, being honest and trustworthy, keeping the channels open and free from obstructions.

"Prayer is not monologue, but a dialogue," said Andrew Murray, known for his insightful writings about powerful prayer. "God's voice in response to mine is its most essential part. Listening to God's voice is the secret of the assurance that He will listen to mine."[5]

When we assume our responsibility in this two-way commitment, our prayer changes from something rote into real communication, into a living relationship with God.

Listening God, I want to dialogue with you all day long today. I want to speak and wait to hear your response. I want our conversations to be like no other communication in my life. Day by day, step by step, help me to build a prayerful relationship with you.

PRAISE
Reveling in the Maker's Character

Praise the LORD.
Praise God in his sanctuary;
praise him in his mighty heavens.
Praise him for his acts of power;
praise him for his surpassing greatness.
Praise him with the sounding of the trumpet,
praise him with the harp and lyre,
praise him with tambourine and dancing,
praise him with the strings and flute,
praise him with the clash of cymbals,
praise him with resounding cymbals.
Let everything that has breath praise the LORD.
Praise the LORD.

—Psalm 150

A basic rule of effective leadership is to catch somebody in the act of doing something well and praise him for it. The same holds true for parenting, developing friendships, managing a workplace—all of our relationships. We thrive on praise. Unless we're in a state of rebellion, we want to know that authority figures approve of us and our actions. Praise builds our self-esteem, confidence, and motivation. It keeps us on track.

God deserves praise, too, but for different reasons. He doesn't need our praise to bolster his esteem or position: we praise him to submit to and appreciate his place in the world. We praise who he is and what he has done for us. We recognize our smallness compared to his greatness and marvel that he stoops to love and work within us. When we praise him, we set aside our needs and reflect on his character. We express love and adoration without expecting anything in return.

"Praise is adoration of God, because of who He is, because He is God. Praise dwells on the attributes of God, the character of God, the being of God, regardless of whether or not God does what we would like to have done. He still is all that the Word of God indicates that He is," explained the preacher Paris Reidhead in *Beyond Petition*.[6]

The biblical psalms are filled with references to God's character, and if we're uncertain how to praise, we can depend on the psalmists for help. For example, Psalm 139 speaks of God as all knowing and ever present. We can use the psalm writer's words to praise God for these attributes, to express what we may find hard to articulate. From the first few verses we can exclaim, "Praise you, God, that you have searched and known me. That you know when I sit and rise, that you perceive my thoughts from afar. I praise you for being all knowing and ever present in my life."

Hopefully, though, we won't always need written guidelines to praise God. We can praise him spontaneously. I'll never forget my uncontrollable outburst when, in my twenties and living as a landlocked Midwesterner, I witnessed the Pacific Ocean for the first time. Driving a rental car, I rounded a tree-lined bend and almost swerved off the road when I encountered the magnificence. The rolling waves so astounded me, I broke into praise: "Praise you, God, for your creation! Praise you for your magnificence! Glory to you for the sights and sounds of the sea! Hallelujah!"

I don't naturally effuse or use language like this, but the grandeur of God flooded my spirit, and I couldn't contain it. After sitting in the car, praising and praying, I drove to my destination, feeling indescribably alive and refreshed.

When we praise, we also meet with surprise, because praise releases the mystical. After lifting our heads or rising from our knees, we may discover that God has generously praised us by renewing our souls.

I thank you, God, for the gift of praise. Today I praise you for your glory, creativity, and magnificence as expressed through nature. I love and adore who you are and what you've created.

SILENCE
Lingering in God's Presence

My heart is not proud, O LORD,
my eyes are not haughty;
I do not concern myself with great matters
or things too wonderful for me.
But I have stilled and quieted my soul;
like a weaned child with its mother,
like a weaned child is my soul within me.
O Israel, put your hope in the LORD
both now and forevermore.

—Psalm 131

I'm a person who likes checking off her to-do list, so I'm tempted to race through prayer as another item to tackle rather than as an engrossing conversation with a dear friend. I'm uncomfortable when I've managed prayer this way, though. I don't even treat my friends the way I sometimes approach God.

With a trusted friend, there are moments of lingering silence between us. Yet the silence doesn't matter; we're so well acquainted, we're secure in each other's presence. I would like to reach this place in prayer with God: to stay silent and longingly enjoy his presence.

Toward this goal, I'm convicted, encouraged, and motivated by words from Andrew Murray, a man who prayed fervently and frequently. Murray wrote, "When man in his littleness and God in His glory meet, we all understand that what God says has infinitely more worth than what man says. And yet our prayer so often consists in the utterance of our thoughts of what we need, that we give God no time to speak to us. Our prayers are often so indefinite and vague. It is a great lesson to learn, that to be silent unto God is the secret of true adoration. Let us remember this promise: 'In quietness and confidence shall be your strength.'

"It is as the soul bows itself before Him to remember His greatness and His holiness, His power and His love, and seeks to give Him the honor and the reverence and the worship that are His due, that the heart will be opened to receive the divine impression of the nearness of God and the working of His power.

"O Christians, do believe that such worship of God—in which you bow low and ever lower in your nothingness, and lift up your thoughts to realize God's presence, as He gives Himself to you in Christ Jesus—is the sure way to give Him the glory that is His due, and will lead to the highest blessedness to be found in prayer.

"Do not imagine that it is time lost. Do not turn from it, if at first it appears difficult or fruitless. Be assured that it brings you into the right relation to God. It opens the way to fellowship with Him. It leads to the blessed assurance that He is looking on you in tender love and working in you with a secret but divine power.

"And as at length you become more accustomed to it, it will give you the sense of His presence abiding with you all the day. It will make you strong to testify for God. Someone has said, 'No one is able to influence others for goodness and holiness beyond the amount that there is of God in him.' Men will begin to feel that you have been with God.

"'The Lord is in His holy temple; be silent before Him, all the earth.

"'Be silent, O all flesh, before the Lord; for He is raised up out of His holy habitation.'"[7]

Lord, I approach you longingly and lovingly, ready to sit silently with you. Whether or not you speak to me, I will adore you and enjoy our time together. Keep me awake and sensitive to your presence. Later let others tell by my peaceful countenance that I have been with you.

PART SIX

HEARING

Listening to His Voice

Lord, speak to me, that I may speak
In living echoes of Thy tone;
As Thou hast sought, so let me seek
Thy erring children lost and lone.

O teach me, Lord, that I may teach
The precious things Thou dost impart;
And wing my words, that they may reach
The hidden depth of many a heart.

O fill me with Thy fullness, Lord,
Until my very heart o'er-flow
In kindling thought and glowing word,
Thy love to tell, Thy praise to show.

O use me, Lord, use even me,
Just as Thou wilt, and when, and where;
Until Thy blessed face I see,
Thy rest, Thy joy, Thy glory share.

"LORD, SPEAK TO ME"
BY FRANCES R. HAVERGAL AND ROBERT SCHUMANN

In his novel *Whalesong,* Robert Siegel weaves an endearing and imaginative tale about a family of humpback whales. A few pages into the novel the reader learns that whales are good listeners. They listen intently for communication, in the form of a song, from other members of the pod.

A young whale, the story's narrator, describes his mother's song: "Each whale had his own song, but none, I thought, equal to my mother's. Hers lasted a long while, beginning with a soft croon to which I'd sometimes fall asleep. Soon, however, it changed into trilling whistles like birds skipping about on a barnacled back or water that leaps and dances down a cliff, then to a long shivery moan that probed every sea cavern between us and the ice at the end of the world.

"This moan stretched and bent in every direction, sometimes higher, sometimes lower, and was the sweetest sound I'd ever listened to. Sometimes it reduced me to tears—I don't know why. Last there followed a series of creaks and clicking noises, very sharp and fetching, which ended in a long whistle. At that my mother would listen for my father's answer. All the pod would listen as one."[1]

Siegel's whales listen to locate one another, to navigate while traveling in groups, and to ensure protection against attackers. They listen as an expression of love and as a means to preserve families and communities. For me they illustrate that throughout the animal kingdom, listening plays a crucial role to survival.

I've seen these marine mammals spout water and jump playfully off the East Coast, but I really only need the backyard to watch creatures listening. Birds flutter and fly when my cat slinks nearby;

the cat perks her ears and hides when a dog approaches; the dog listens for car sounds before crossing a street. Observing nature's instincts, I wonder, *Why is it so hard for people to listen, to do what even the animals know is important for survival?*

We might try to hear one another, we may even occasionally listen to our own souls, but we often neglect listening to God. Yet he is the one we depend on for physical and spiritual survival, the one who woos and nurtures, warns and corrects, guides and sustains us. So why won't we listen? Why don't we hear?

Perhaps we don't understand that he is the voice of compassion and protection. We don't realize he is the comforter, the giver of good gifts, the ever-attentive lover of our souls. He is not the distant father, the critical mother, the man who emotionally or physically left us. He is God and God is love.

Yes, it must be a misunderstanding. We must be confusing him with somebody else. Why else would we be too busy or afraid to listen? (Why else would we let the animals be smarter than us?) Why else would we refuse the sound of love?

BASIC INSTINCTS

Thoughts on Sensing the Right Way

I will listen to what God the LORD will say;
he promises peace to his people, his saints—
but let them not return to folly.
Surely his salvation is near those who fear him,
that his glory may dwell in our land. . . .
The LORD will indeed give what is good,
and our land will yield its harvest.
Righteousness goes before him
and prepares the way for his steps.

—Psalm 85:8–9, 12–13

Often, hearing God's voice isn't as difficult as we imagine it to be. In fact, sometimes his voice rings so clear that we miss following it; we can't believe he'd be so straightforward. As with most lessons in my life, I learned this the hard way and embarrassed myself.

I'd been invited to dinner at a single mom's house, and the offer touched me. I knew Elaine didn't have much money, but she wanted to share from her modest supply. What an honor; what an expression of purely motivated giving!

On the way to Elaine's I stopped at the grocery store, and while walking to the checkout counter, the words *flowers* and *bubble gum* popped into my mind. *That's weird,* I thought. *Why would I suddenly think of these items?* I debated for a few moments. *Could this be God's voice telling me something? Am I supposed to take flowers and bubble gum to my friend's home?*

Finally I decided, *No, it can't be.* I didn't think the message was mystical enough to be from God. Certainly he wouldn't sound so concise and practical, and I doubted he'd involve himself with such minutiae. I left the grocery store and soon entered my friend's house empty-handed.

Somewhere in our conversation that evening, I mentioned my strange message, and Elaine looked astonished. "Wow, my favorite gift is fresh flowers, and my son absolutely loves bubble gum," she said gently, letting me off the hook. I felt stunned. It had been God talking to me, wanting to express his great love for Elaine through small gifts.

That incident changed my thinking about hearing God's voice. To get our attention he rarely appears and says, "Thus saith the Lord." Rather, in the course of daily life he enters our thought processes and impresses our hearts with his messages. Frequently they are messages to "do good" to others.

Still, if I'm doubtful a message originates with God, I try to follow these basic guidelines: If a thought or inner impression encourages me to do good, then I do it; if the message compels me to do harm, then I don't do it. I often remind myself of the Lord's instruction, "In everything, do to others what you would have them do to you" and follow the inner advice, even if I risk missing the mark or looking foolish.

I still don't "get it right" every time, but I think that discerning God's voice is a lifelong learning process rather than a crash course. And in the end I'd rather hear him say "At least you tried," instead of "Why didn't you listen?"

Besides, hearing and following his voice isn't just a way to bless others. It fills and enlarges the soul of the giver, too. How like God to create communication that spiritually benefits and encourages the giver as well as the receiver! How like God to show us in small and quiet ways the depth and breadth of his love.

Father, forgive me for the times I've missed your instructions. Help me to discern your voice and "do good" when I'm prompted to do it. Thank you for taking the time to speak to me and use my ability to give for your kingdom.

THE MEMORY OF HIS WORDS

The Creator Writes with Indelible Ink

Your commands make me wiser than my enemies,
for they are ever with me.
I have more insight than all my teachers,
for I meditate on your statutes.
I have more understanding than the elders,
for I obey your precepts. . . .
How sweet are your words to my taste,
sweeter than honey to my mouth!
I gain understanding from your precepts;
therefore I hate every wrong path.

—Psalm 119:98–100, 103–104

I grew up in a back-to-basics church, and if there's one thing I learned, it was a respect for the Scriptures. In Sunday morning and evening services, at Wednesday night prayer meetings and weekly home Bible studies, during vacation Bible school and annual revival conferences, we immersed ourselves in God's Word.

We also memorized Bible verses and passages, and for several years I was the reigning Scripture Memory Queen of the children's Sunday school program. I'd like to say I memorized Bible verses out of a deep love for God, but looking back, I think it appealed most to my competitive spirit. I loved winning prizes and proving I was the best.

I particularly remember working hard to memorize verses when the first-place prize for Scripture memory was a bride doll. The moment I saw her inside a cellophane-wrapped box, sitting on top of the church basement's piano, I knew she was mine. No small prizes would do. I memorized every word and reference perfectly and, of course, more verses than anyone else. The beautiful doll went home with me.

Though I've never asked my mother, I suspect she detected my selfish motives. As I recited verses to her during home practice sessions, she probably thought, *Well, at least it's a way to get Scripture into my daughter's mind, and maybe it will sink into her heart.*

Later as a young adult, I abandoned my faith (or at least tried to), but wherever I went, whatever I did, the Scriptures tagged along with me. I remember sitting at a party, watching friends take drugs, get drunk, pair off in couples, and head toward privacy. I wanted to join in, but as soon as I entertained the thought, a Bible verse from my childhood marched annoyingly across my brain. *Oh brother,* I thought, *I can't even enjoy sin like everybody else. I know too much about the Bible!* God had written his words in my soul, and even when I closed my ears, my heart heard them speak.

After several difficult years I returned to Christ, and the Scriptures immediately sprang up in my soul as if they'd stowed away, waiting for that moment. I like to tell mothers this story to encourage them in teaching their young ones Scripture or to strengthen their hope for a spiritually wayward child. They may never know when God's voice, via a childhood Bible verse, will pop up to guide, protect, or convict their children.

That's the remarkable power of Scripture. However it enters our lives, it's nearly impossible to eradicate its message from our soul. The memory of his words is God's surefire way of communicating with us when we don't know where else to turn or, in some cases, if we're trying to avoid listening. And for this, I am grateful.

Thank you, God, for the power of your words through the Scriptures. Please speak to me today not only when I read the Bible but also as I work or play. I want to love your law and meditate on it all the day.

LISTENING FOR HARMONY
Identifying God-Inspired Communication

With my lips I recount
    all the laws that come from your mouth.
I rejoice in following your statutes
    as one rejoices in great riches.
I meditate on your precepts
    and consider your ways.
I delight in your decrees;
    I will not neglect your word.
Do good to your servant, and I will live;
    I will obey your word.
Open my eyes that I may see
    wonderful things in your law.

—Psalm 119:13–18

Family members might disagree because they've listened to my retold stories, but I believe good advice is worth repeating.

The best insights I've gleaned about listening for God's voice derive from Hannah Whitall Smith's classic book *The Christian's Secret of a Happy Life* published in 1870. I've dispensed some of her advice in another book I've published, but since Hannah's work has sold over two million copies, she's certainly worth repeating.

In regard to hearing God's voice, Hannah first directed Christians to the Bible. She wrote, "The Bible, it is true, does not always give a rule for every particular course of action, and in these cases we need and must expect guidance in other ways. But the Scriptures are far more explicit, even about details, than most people think, and there are not many important affairs in life for which a clear direction may not be found in God's book. . . .

"If therefore, you find yourself in perplexity, first of all search and see whether the Bible speaks on a point in question, asking God to make plain to you, by the power of His Spirit, through the Scriptures, what is His mind. And whatever shall seem to you to be plainly taught there, that you must obey. No special guidance will ever be given about a point on which the Scriptures are explicit, nor could any guidance ever be contrary to the Scriptures."

Hannah then recommended "the test of harmony" for discerning God's guidance. She advised, "We come now to the question as to how God's guidance is to come to us, and how we shall be able to know His voice. There are four ways in which He reveals His will to us—through the Scriptures [an idea worth repeating!], through providential circumstances, through the conviction of our own higher judgment, and through the impressions of the Holy Spirit on our minds. Where these four harmonize, it is to say that God speaks.

"For I lay it down as a foundation principle, which no one can gainsay, that of course His voice will always be in harmony with itself, no matter in how many different ways He may speak. The voices may be many, the message can be but one.

"If God tells me in one voice to do or to leave undone anything, He cannot possibly tell me the opposite in another voice. If there is a contradiction in the voices, the speakers cannot be the same. Therefore my rule for distinguishing the voice of God would be to bring it to the test of this harmony."[2]

I couldn't have said it better myself.

I will search the Scriptures for your guidance, God, then listen for harmony in the ways you talk to me. Sharpen my spiritual ears so I can hear the words you speak to my soul.

MERCIFUL MESSAGES

Hearing from God When Trouble Descends

The LORD is gracious and righteous;
  our God is full of compassion.
The LORD protects the simplehearted;
  when I was in great need, he saved me.
Be at rest once more, O my soul,
  for the LORD has been good to you.
For you, O LORD, have delivered my soul
    from death,
  my eyes from tears,
  my feet from stumbling,
that I may walk before the LORD
  in the land of the living.

—Psalm 116:5–9

Today at the beauty salon I talked with a woman who's been notified she'll lose her job soon because of middle-management cutbacks.

"I should have known this was coming," she said.

"What do you mean?" I asked.

"Well, a few weeks ago I felt God kept saying to me, 'Sell everything.' So I began cleaning out my cluttered basement and taking things I don't need to the auction."

I was curious. "How did you know he was telling you that?" I asked.

"I just kept getting those words repeated in my head," she said. "So I'm taking by faith that it's God telling me. Before he said to sell everything, I also started getting *the verse* he always gives me when my life is about to get difficult."

Still curious, I asked, "How did that happen?"

"Well, the same verse kept showing up everywhere. At Bible study, on the radio, in conversations—and a friend gave me a journal with that verse on the front cover! Then after getting this verse delivered to me various ways, I found out I'd lose my job."

The verse was Jeremiah 29:11: "'For I know the plans I have for you,' declares the LORD, 'plans to prosper you and not to harm you, plans to give you hope and a future.'"

C. S. Lewis wrote that "God whispers to us in our pleasure, speaks in our conscience, and shouts in our pain."[3] In Darleen's case, he is shouting ahead of time, preparing her for the coming days. I hope she also remembers the promises following her recurring verse from God. Jeremiah 29:12–13 promises, "Then you will call upon me and come and pray to me, and I will listen to you. You will seek me and find me when you seek me with all your heart."

Though I know that the days ahead won't be easy, I'm excited for Darleen. She's receiving God's merciful messages—his assurance that he'll provide for her, that she'll pass through the transition with an unscathed soul. He's preparing her to walk through anxiety with her head and heart held up, and I anticipate something better for Darleen in the days to come.

When we're anticipating trying times—or we're already mired in the middle of difficulty—God employs unusual measures to get our attention and remind us that he's always present and ready to help. He can shout louder than pain, but we still must listen and follow.

Hopefully, the next time God shouts at me I'll remember Darleen's example and begin my own version of "selling everything." How about you?

You are the Great Communicator. Please shout to me when I'm in pain or if there are trying days ahead. I want to consider your attention-grabbing shouts as merciful messages from a Father who will provide for and watch over me during difficulty.

CRIES AND WHISPERS

Nurturing a Soft Conscience

Who may ascend the hill of the LORD?
  Who may stand in his holy place?
He who has clean hands and a pure heart,
  who does not lift up his soul to an idol
  or swear by what is false.
He will receive blessing from the LORD
  and vindication from God his Savior.

—Psalm 24:3–5

In a short story titled "Good Country People," Flannery O'Connor created a quirky traveling Bible salesman who visited a rural community. While peddling Bibles, the salesman insisted, "The word of God ought to be in the parlor. . . . For a Christian, the word of God ought to be in every room in the house besides in his heart."

However, upon opening his valise in front of a young girl, the salesman revealed a box of condoms, a flask of whiskey, and an obscene deck of cards.

One day as two women knelt in a back pasture digging up onions, they saw the salesman emerge from the woods and walk toward the highway.

"Why, that looks like the nice dull young man that tried to sell me a Bible yesterday," said Mrs. Hopewell. "He was so simple. I guess the world would be better off if we were all that simple."

"Some can't be that simple," replied her companion, Mrs. Freeman. "I know I never could."[4]

Without knowing about the salesman's valise and his unsavory activities in the woods, Mrs. Freeman understood human nature and its duplicity. On the outside we might exhibit virtue, but inside we can be stocked with sin. We may tote Bibles, but we can still harbor dull consciences and hardened hearts. Consequently, we muffle the cries and whispers of the Holy Spirit speaking to us.

Paul emphasized the importance of a clear conscience in communication with God. He told the Christian Hebrews, "Let us draw near to God with a sincere heart in full assurance of faith, having our hearts sprinkled to cleanse us from a guilty conscience and having our bodies washed with pure water." Evidently, a clear conscience assists our ability to talk to God and listen for his reply.

Conversely, a guilty conscience prompts us to avoid God; we shrink from his light and retreat to a dark corner for comfort. We fear that if we expose our rebellion to him, we're in for punishment, but this is a false assumption. God asks that we approach him with our stiff heart and conscience, handing them over for repair and softening, letting him clean their inner channels so we can hear him again.

At one point during my spiritual defection, I realized my heart had grown so hard that I couldn't soften it on my own. I knew I couldn't get back to God through my efforts. "Lord, I can't return by my own strength," I prayed. "If you want me back, you'll need to do it." The Lord accepted that admission as a small step toward him, and gradually he softened my "impossibly" hard heart without any assistance.

Living with a pure soul often necessitates that we do the opposite of what we're inclined to do. When a guilty conscience suggests fleeing God's presence, it's an opportune time to run toward him, requesting his grace. He doesn't wait for us with a big stick. He tarries with open, forgiving arms.

Holy Spirit, even though my conscience is guilty and my heart feels hard, I will run to you, asking for grace and forgiveness. Please pardon me, cleanse me, and make me new.

MINISTRY OF THE EARS

Listening to Spiritual Seekers

Hear, O LORD, my righteous plea;
  listen to my cry.
Give ear to my prayer—
  it does not rise from deceitful lips. . . .
I call on you, O God, for you will answer me;
  give ear to me and hear my prayer. . . .
And I—in righteousness I will see your face;
  when I awake, I will be satisfied with seeing
    your likeness.

—Psalm 17:1, 6, 15

I couldn't believe my ears.

Out of all the people in the office, she chose me as the person most likely to listen. Feeling caught off guard and trapped, I surrendered and reluctantly listened . . . and listened . . . and listened. I listened for days, weeks, months. Some days her pain and questioning overwhelmed me, but I still listened. I didn't know what else to do.

Then to my surprise, all of the ear-tiring service paid off. One day she stopped long enough to ask me about Jesus. I uttered a few words about sin and salvation, and she became a Christian. And quite unexpectedly I'd discovered "the ministry of the ears."

A few years and several listening relationships later, I learned more about this low-key method of introducing people to God. As I suspected, I wasn't the first to practice a listening ministry. Long before me, a frustrated but determined Japanese evangelist carefully developed a listening technique he called "the evangelism of the ears."

After spending much time earnestly spreading the gospel to his countrymen, the evangelist decided to follow up on his converts. To his dismay, few of those under his preaching who were professing salvation had remained committed to Christ. Deeply discouraged by such poor results, he discarded his evangelistic itinerary and began talking to people face-to-face. It was a radical step. After all, people never expected a preacher to *listen* to them.

Eventually the new method worked. By listening, the evangelist communicated Christ's love in a concrete way. In the end he produced enduring followers of Christ, not just temporary professions based on emotional whims.[5]

My motives for listening to a distraught secretary, though they were not as pure as the evangelist's, led me to unwittingly convey the right message. Without words, listening to a hurting person said "I care" and led her to God. I'm especially interested in this method because during my years away from God, the Christians who listened influenced me back to the kingdom, not those who talked or preached at me. I believe that this "ministry of the ears" models God's example: he hears and listens, then speaks in a still, small voice. He is the gentleman lover who woos us carefully.

Listening and hearing, then, is another way we can be like Christ. He hears us with the desire that afterward we listen to and follow him. "Give ear and come to me," says the Lord. "Hear me, that your soul may live." It seems not only fair but faithful that we listen in return. Not only for his sake but for the sake of our souls.

Thank you for listening to and hearing me. Thank you for wooing me with your gentleness. Oh, God, help me to remember that communication isn't a one-sided blathering on my part. I will listen to you in return and follow what you say.

PART SEVEN

REFLECTING

Developing a Discerning Mind

Take Thou our minds, dear Lord, we humbly pray;
Give us the mind of Christ each passing day;
Teach us to know the truth that sets us free;
Grant us in all our thoughts to honor Thee.

Take Thou our hearts, O Christ, they are Thine own;
Come Thou within our souls and claim Thy throne;
Help us to shed abroad Thy deathless love;
Use us to make the earth like heav'n above.

Take Thou ourselves, O Lord, heart, mind, and will;
Through our surrendered souls Thy plans fulfill.
We yield ourselves to Thee—time, talents, all!
We hear, and henceforth heed Thy sovereign call.

"TAKE THOU OUR MINDS, DEAR LORD"
BY WILLIAM H. FOULKES AND CALVIN W. LAUFER

Charles Steinmetz, the electrical theorist and inventor, was called out of retirement to solve a baffling breakdown of machinery at General Electric. Despite concerted efforts, none of GE's engineers could pinpoint the cause.

After his arrival Steinmetz walked around the massive machinery complex, testing various parts. Then he took a piece of chalk out of his pocket and marked a part of one machine. The engineers disassembled the machine and to their surprise found the defect exactly where Steinmetz left his mark.

A few days later GE received a bill for $10,000 from Steinmetz. The company protested, asking him to itemize the costs. He sent back this statement:

Making one chalk mark $1.00
Knowing where to place the mark $9,999.00[1]

It's one thing to have knowledge; it's another thing to understand and correctly apply it.

So it is with our soul's development. We can learn about shaping the soul but never effectively apply the principles to our lives. More specifically, we can know about God but never learn to think from his viewpoint.

To distinguish what's good for the soul, to think from God's vantage point, requires discernment. The apostle Paul explained that the Holy Spirit helps us understand the Creator's mind—as much as humans are permitted to comprehend it. The Spirit searches God's mind and helps us think his thoughts if we're open to receiving and believing them.

Paul told the Corinthians, "The man without the Spirit does not accept the things that come from the Spirit of God, for they are foolishness to him, and he cannot understand them, because they are spiritually discerned." Then he added, "But we have the mind of Christ."

We have the mind of Christ! What a priceless treasure; what a valuable resource!

With Christ's mind-set we step deeper into the soul life, taking in information and discerning whether the message or "truths" originate with God. Tapped into the supernatural, we can distinguish between the spiritual and carnal—and with confidence know where to leave our mark in the world.

EATING GOD'S WORDS

Feasting on His Viewpoint

The law of the LORD is perfect,
  reviving the soul.
The statutes of the LORD are trustworthy,
  making wise the simple.
The precepts of the LORD are right,
  giving joy to the heart.
The commands of the LORD are radiant,
  giving light to the eyes.
The fear of the LORD is pure,
  enduring forever.
The ordinances of the LORD are sure
  and altogether righteous.

—Psalm 19:7–9

Gertrude Stein, famous for her experimental prose and well-argued lectures, drove her old Model-T Ford to a garage, expecting prompt repairs. A young man who'd just returned from World War I serviced her car.

The repairman was inept—or at least didn't make Miss Stein's car a top priority. The garage owner reprimanded the young man, and the author coined her famous phrase: "All of you young people who served in the war—you are a lost generation."

Later when Gertrude lay dying from cancer, she murmured to a friend at her bedside, "What is the answer?" Her friend remained silent. The dying woman persisted and countered, "In that case, what is the question?"[2]

During her life, Gertrude Stein concocted creative answers for everything and everyone, but facing death she, too, was lost. Her clever thinking hadn't been rooted in the eternal, in God's redemptive viewpoint, in spiritual truths that dwell in his heart.

The Scriptures offer a fundamental way to capture God's thinking; by reading and reflecting on them, we feed not only the mind but the whole soul. Jesus declared, "I am the bread of life. He who comes to me will never go hungry, and he who believes in me will never be thirsty. . . . For I have come down from heaven not to do my will but to do the will of him who sent me."

To chastise the hardened hearts and minds around him, Jesus added, "But as I told you, you have seen me and still you do not believe." It's possible to feast from God, to handle the bread of life, and still not ingest his holy mind-set.

In most cultures wheat and its familiar product, bread, is considered the "staff of life." To emphasize their necessity, some nutritionists call wheat and grains "brain foods." Wheat is the world's largest food crop and provides more nourishment to people than anything else they intake. Remarkably, if wheat production were evenly distributed throughout the earth, every person could receive one-third of the required daily calories and half the protein by eating bread.

Wheat is a nutrient-dense food and can override nutritional deficiencies in Western diets, too. Only four of the forty-four essential nutrients are missing from whole wheat. The problem, however, is that the Western world processes most of the nutrients out of whole wheat. Refined flour lacks eighty percent of the nutrients existing in the original kernel.[3]

Accordingly, we can "refine" the Scriptures so we eat only part of them rather than swallowing all of what God intends for us to know and do. We digest only what tastes good to us. I've been guilty of this. I've read favorite passages that comfort me and confirm my opinions and have avoided Scriptures that convict or challenge me. Hopefully, admitting this will prompt me to change my spiritual eating habits.

Without reservation, Jeremiah, a prophet who knew God's mind, told the Lord, "When your words came, I ate them; they were my joy and my heart's delight, for I bear your name, O LORD God Almighty." This unreserved eating nourishes the soul from God's heart and mind, filling us with his desires and viewpoint.

Bread of Life, I will feast on all that you offer in the Scriptures. I confess my "refining" your words to fit my viewpoint instead of fattening my soul with your pure truths. Lord, when your words come, I will eat all of them.

A MIND OF YOUR OWN
Respecting Internal Processes

LORD, who may dwell in your sanctuary?
 Who may live on your holy hill?
He whose walk is blameless
 and who does what is righteous,
who speaks the truth from his heart....
The fear of the LORD is the beginning of
  wisdom;
 all who follow his precepts have good
  understanding.
 To him belongs eternal praise.

—Psalm 15:1–2; 111:10

When Johnny Carson first signed on for *The Tonight Show,* so many reporters wanted interviews that the comedian responded with his usual humor. He created this list of answers to which journalists could provide the questions:

1. Yes, I did.
2. Not a bit of truth to that rumor.
3. Only twice in my life, both times on Saturday.
4. I can do either, but I prefer the first.

5. No. Kumquats.
6. I can't answer that question.
7. Toads and tarantulas.
8. Turkestan, Denmark, Chile, and the Komandorskie Islands.
9. As often as possible, but I'm not very good at it yet.
10. It happened to some old friends of mine, and I'll never forget it.[4]

Some days I wish life could reduce to ten pat answers for everything, but God doesn't operate that way. Nor should we. He's gifted us with minds to think, discern, and choose how we'll walk in his ways and speak truth from our hearts. We're to stand alone before God apart from husbands, pastors, parents, friends, or other spiritual influencers, and individually inspect our souls.

This is not a rebellious statement against those in authority but a reminder that we're to respect our internal processes and think for ourselves. We can share these thoughts with others, change our minds based on their input, even choose to submit when we don't fully agree, but God never asks us to stop exercising our minds.

In her book *Every Woman's Privilege,* Joy Gage warns, "Women receive direction through many channels today—the local church, Christian books, Christian radio and television, a favorite tape ministry, or even self-appointed spiritual gurus. By whatever vehicle the message comes, if a woman allows it to define her personal accountability, she will become confused over spiritual goals. It is our responsibility to practice discernment as listeners—to filter the messages received."[5]

This advice appears obvious, but, without realizing it, we can grow lazy about thinking for ourselves. We can follow the latest fads. Or we can succumb to subtle messages that our opinions, intuitions, and thinking patterns are inferior or marginal. Bit by bit we can shut up and shut down, surrendering our brains to others and eventually depleting our souls.

Throughout Scripture God asks us to make choices; to renew, gird up, and guard our minds; to be like-minded with Christ. But he never asks us to stop using our brains. Consequently, when we're tempted to discount thinking for ourselves, we can remember that even though we surrender to him, God still reserves our right to gather information, process it, and make decisions.

And if God never discounts our minds, why should anyone else?

I will use my mind to gather information, process it for spiritual truth, and decide how to live for you, Lord. Thank you for the gift of thinking. Guard me against throwing it away. Teach me how to use this gift wisely in a way that grows my soul.

ARTFUL OBEDIENCE
The Power of an Unequivocal Yes

Test me, O LORD, and try me,
 examine my heart and my mind;
for your love is ever before me,
 and I walk continually in your truth. . . .
I lead a blameless life;
 redeem me and be merciful to me.
My feet stand on level ground;
 in the great assembly I will praise the LORD.

Psalm 26:2–3, 11–12

The words must have plundered Abram's soul. "Leave your country, your relatives, your father's house," said the Lord. "I'm taking you to another land, and there I'll make you great among nations."

The part about greatness sounded good, but leave his homeland, his relatives? His was a patriarchal culture, a continuum of tightly knit families—and age seventy-five was hardly a convenient time to uproot.

Still, Abram chose to obey God no matter what and once Abram pointed his sandals away from home, the trouble began. Famine engulfed the land; Pharaoh lusted after Abram's wife, Sarai; his herdsmen squabbled incessantly; he lost part of his real estate to Lot, who was later captured by warring kings (Abram rescued him); and Sarai continually grieved due to maternal barrenness. All the while, the Lord pulled Abram aside to say, "Look at the land; look at the stars. Your descendants will be greater than these. I am your shield. Your reward will be very great."

About then a warm bowl of porridge shared with family in his old hometown seemed the real blessing, but Abram believed God. His faith was counted to him as righteousness, and at age one hundred, bearing the new name "Abraham," he begat Isaac.

God could have blessed Abraham without dragging him through the desert to face wretched weather and hostile nations, but he wanted an unequivocal yes before bestowing the great rewards. With the command to leave family—a command that included the near sacrifice of Isaac several years later—God artfully tested Abraham's faith, love, and obedience.

For following God's plan, Abraham was rewarded with God's equally artful blessing. Abraham's family circle was eventually enlarged, and he became the father of many nations. Not surprisingly, God's great blessing was one that Abraham couldn't outlive. Its power and influence continued long past Abraham's earthly travels and his very life; it has never ended.

"And if we answer the call to discipleship, where will it lead us? What decisions and partings will it demand?" asked Dietrich Bonhoeffer centuries later. "To answer this question we shall have to go to him, for only he knows the answer. Only Jesus Christ, who bids us follow him, knows the journey's end. But we do know that it will be a road of boundless mercy. Discipleship means joy."[6]

Obedience also produces joy when we realize the power of an unequivocal yes. We may not fully comprehend God's plans as we pass through them, but with mindful reflection, we can look back and feel relieved and thankful that we obeyed.

Søren Kierkegaard said, "Life can only be understood backwards; but it must be lived forwards."[7] This is especially true for people who choose to artfully obey God.

God of Abraham and Isaac, I need the courage to artfully obey you. Please give me your encouragement, perhaps a special promise that motivates me to obey when I don't fully understand your plans.

SORTING OUT
Filtering Life Through the Soul

I am always with you;
you hold me by my right hand.
You guide me with your counsel,
and afterward you will take me into glory.
Whom have I in heaven but you?
And earth has nothing I desire besides you.
My flesh and my heart may fail,
but God is the strength of my heart
and my portion forever.

—Psalm 73:23–26

Tonight I feel grieved. This last year several friends have chosen spiritually compromising pathways, and their life-altering choices could lead them away from God. Time will expose the validity of my concern, but for these moments I let myself feel sad and wonder, *What in the world went wrong?*

All of these women profess faith in Christ; they all understand the necessity of growing the soul. Yet as I reflect on each woman's decision and reasons for it, I uncover a common thread of misunderstanding. They have mistaken their personal feelings for filtering life through the soul. "I feel good about this," said one friend. "I don't feel guilty about my choice," explained another. "This feels right for me," concluded another, dismissing my questions.

I'm a proponent of soul-based living, but I don't believe that soulish choices, especially life-changing decisions, depend on emotions. It's possible to sin and feel good about it or feel nothing at all. Rather, when we sort out our desires and search for answers, we can ask ourselves the following questions:

How does it line up with Scripture? If our decision contradicts God's will according to the Bible, the search ends. God stated his moral laws in the Scriptures; disobeying them is sin. It's amazing how frequently the root of our decisions leads back to the Ten Commandments or other plainly expressed directives.

What has God spoken to me personally? After Scripture, how has God spoken to us personally in the past? Are we following or neglecting his specific communication now?

How will this affect me spiritually? A couple of women said, "I don't think this will affect me at all spiritually," when describing a willful choice to sin. Again, answering this question doesn't depend on our thinking or feeling but on what God says.

Will this fatten or wither my soul? A decision may pass the morality test, but the resulting actions could deplete our inner peace and resources. If we take this direction, will we still tend to the soul? Will we have time to spend with God? Do we sense any reservations within?

After the basic questions, we can add these queries if we understand our life mission, our personal and God-given reason for being:

Will I stay authentic to who God created me to be? Will we be trying to become someone we're not? Are we bending to pressure from others to feel, think, and do what they want? On the other hand, are we confusing rebellion with "being true to ourselves"?

Does this contribute to my purpose in life? Does this choice move us toward or away from our life goal? Does it help us focus on a long-range purpose rather than short-term gratification? A year or more from today, how will this choice affect us?

All questions considered, the bottom line is this: Are we fully involving God in our choices as we filter them through the soul? If so, to thrive spiritually we may not need to answer any of these questions, or we could feel compelled to explore them all. Whatever the case, don't begrudge the time and reflection these questions require. After all, a soul is a terrible thing to waste.

Lord, you are my Guide. I need honesty as I filter life-changing choices through my soul. I desire your presence and wisdom as I reflect on which pathway to take. Please walk with me through this decision-making process, whispering in my ear about your soul-thriving way.

PART EIGHT

SEEING

Looking Past the Physical World

Open my eyes, that I may see
Glimpses of truth Thou hast for me;
Place in my hands the wonderful key
That shall unclasp and set me free.

Silently now, I wait for Thee,
Ready, my God, Thy will to see;
Open my eyes, illumine me,
Spirit divine!

Open my way, that I may bring,
Trophies of grace to Christ, my King;
Echoed in love Thy word shall out-ring,
Sweet as the note that angels sing.

Silently now I wait for Thee,
Ready, my God, Thy will to see;
Open my way, illumine me,
Spirit divine!

"OPEN MY EYES THAT I MAY SEE"
BY C. H. S. MORRIS, FRED P. MORRIS, AND CLARA H. SCOTT

Just before Christmas in 1863, President Abraham Lincoln dreamed he attended a party of undistinguished people. When they discovered Lincoln's identity, several guests commented on his appearance.

"He's very common looking," someone said.

To this Lincoln replied, "The Lord prefers common-looking people. That's the reason he makes so many of them!"[1] History reveals that Lincoln's "commonness" made him popular with everyday Americans and that his ordinary features lay only skin deep.

As we deepen spiritually, we increasingly look for and appreciate what resides within a person, inside the soul. And as we journey into the world, we view it from a heavenly perspective instead of our own. With the lens of the Holy Spirit, we look past the physical world into its spiritual workings.

Paul prayed that the Ephesians would see with the eyes of the Spirit. He wrote to them, "I keep asking that the God of our Lord Jesus Christ, the glorious Father, may give you the Spirit of wisdom and revelation, so that you may know him better. I pray also that the eyes of your heart may be enlightened in order that you may know the hope to which he has called you, the riches of his glorious inheritance in the saints, and his incomparably great power for us who believe."

It's been said, "Open your eyes and the whole world is full of God."[2] We can request such vision by repeating Peter Marshall's prayer: "Give us open eyes, Father, to see the beauty all around us and to see it in Thy handiwork. Let all lovely things fill us with gladness and let them lift up our hearts in true worship.

"Give us this day, O Lord, a strong and vivid sense that Thou art by our side. By Thy grace, let us go nowhere this day where Thou canst not come nor court any companionship that would rob us of Thine. Through Jesus Christ our Lord. Amen."[3]

ADJUSTING THE EYES

Focusing on Future Treasures

May the LORD answer you when you are in distress;
may the name of the God of Jacob protect you.
May he send you help from the sanctuary
and grant you support from Zion. . . .
Now I know that the LORD saves his anointed;
he answers him from his holy heaven
with the saving power of his right hand.
Some trust in chariots and some in horses,
but we trust in the name of the LORD.

—Psalm 20:1–2, 6–7

In the fifteenth century, Madame Guyon of France was imprisoned for her deep devotion to God. Through the centuries, her autobiography has encouraged and challenged Christians, and it still survives today. It gives testament to the enduring influence of one woman's faith but also to God's abundant ability to use a person wholly committed to him.

About her prison term at Vincennes, Madame Guyon wrote, "I shall not speak of that long persecution, which has made so much noise, for a series of ten years' imprisonments, in all sorts of prisons, and of a banishment almost as long, and not yet ended, through crosses, calumnies, and all imaginable sorts of suffering. These are facts too odious on the part of divers persons, which charity induces me to cover."

Through her ordeals, Madame Guyon never renounced her faith. She viewed her suffering through spiritual eyes, focusing on God's holy and beautiful presence within and around her. Looking beyond the physical world, she transformed torture into hidden treasures for the soul.

"When I was a prisoner at Vincennes, and Monsieur De La Reine examined me, I passed my time in great peace, content to pass the rest of my life there, if such were the will of God. I sang songs of joy, which the maid who served me learned by heart, as fast as I made them. We together sang Thy praises, O my God!" she explained.

"The stones of my prison looked in my eyes like rubies; I esteemed them more than all the gaudy brilliancies of a vain world. My heart was full of that joy which Thou givest to them who love Thee, in the midst of their greatest crosses."[4]

The stones of my prison looked in my eyes like rubies. We can remember this proclamation when disappointment surrounds us. Our prisons may not be literal, but we do reach times of emotional or physical entrapment, and hope lies in exercising our spiritual vision. In these prisons God shapes and polishes our souls into jewels, bright with the reflection of his nature. As we wait for freedom, we can look ahead to the future treasure of a deepened soul, used more expansively by him in ways we can't imagine.

Madame Guyon didn't know that God would preserve her testimony for the ages, that she'd represent "the highest pinnacle of spirituality and Christian devotion."[5] Given loss after loss and sorrow upon sorrow, she did the only thing left within her power to do. She looked with spiritual eyes and discovered rubies.

Dear God, help me to search and find your jewels. Thank you that I am not alone when I feel imprisoned. Show me how to view the walls as rubies, the difficult times as hidden treasures for the soul. As I wait for a better tomorrow, please shape and polish me so I reflect your nature.

TRUSTING THE UNSEEN

Believing in the Soul's Truth

Set a guard over my mouth, O LORD;
  keep watch over the door of my lips.
Let not my heart be drawn to what is evil,
  to take part in wicked deeds
with men who are evildoers. . . .
But my eyes are fixed on you, O Sovereign LORD;
  in you I take refuge. . . .
Surely you desire truth in the inner parts;
  you teach me wisdom in the inmost place.

—Psalm 141:3–4, 8; 51:6

As I hesitantly opened the front door, I recognized the spectacled youngster on my porch as a new neighbor from the condo downstairs. I didn't know much about her except that she lived with her mother.

Earlier that day I'd seen the girl riding a bike on our mutual sidewalk. After eyeing her clashing shorts, shirt, and socks, I wondered what kind of mother would unleash this outfit on an unsuspecting neighborhood. Now the fashion fiasco stood inches away, thrusting a folded note into my hands. It read: *I am your new neighbor downstairs, and I need your help. I have the flu, and my daughter Mallory has only eaten a sandwich today. Could you please take her to McDonald's for a Happy Meal and to the store to get ice and crackers? Thanks. Amanda.*

"Of course," I told Mallory. "Go tell your mom it's okay, and I'll get ready." Mallory chattered about her mother's illness and then hopped down the outside stairs. I rummaged for my car keys and thought, *Weird clothes. No food. Sending her daughter out with a stranger. What kind of mother is Amanda?*

Mallory and I drove off together, and after a few blocks the funky outfit faded from my judgmental vision. She filled our conversation with tidbits about her nine-year-old life and interests, and by the time she nibbled a burger and fries, Mallory had boggled me with information about weather patterns, the space shuttle, and our local economy.

This kid is really something . . . much more informed than any fourth-grader I've met before, I thought. Then I mentally chided myself for concluding that mismatched clothes meant mixed-up mothering. I wanted to meet the woman responsible for Mallory.

A few days later Amanda knocked on my door to thank me for helping her daughter.

"My pleasure," I replied. "She's so mature, she's got to be nine years old going on nineteen. Mallory's a special little girl."

"I think so," she smiled.

Over the next weeks I observed Amanda as an attentive, creative, loving mother and undeserving of my hasty, critical impressions. I'd mistakenly assessed a few physical qualities instead of acquainting myself with her soul. (An irony, because Amanda gave me latitude by trusting me with her daughter!) Without knowing it, Amanda reminded me to delve into the truth about people, the truth dwelling within them, rather than what floats on the surface. She reminded me that God asks us to see and relate to what resides in the heart.

When Samuel searched for a king to anoint, the Lord cautioned, "The LORD does not look at the things man looks at. Man looks at the outward appearance, but the LORD looks at the heart." The Lord looks at what molds the soul.

Look at what resides in my soul, God, and purge what doesn't reflect your truth. Then from a pure heart I can see people with spiritual eyes rather than judge their outward appearances.

A SINGLE VISION

Keeping Eyes on the Goal

I will be careful to lead a blameless life—
    when will you come to me?
I will walk in my house
    with blameless heart.
I will set before my eyes
    no vile thing.
The deeds of faithless men I hate;
    they will not cling to me. . . .
My eyes will be on the faithful in the land,
    that they may dwell with me;
he whose walk is blameless
    will minister to me.

—Psalm 101:2–3, 6

In 1868 Louisa May Alcott wrote in her diary, "Began the second part of *Little Women.* I can do a chapter a day, and in a month I mean to be done. A little success is so inspiring that I now find my 'Marches' [a family in her novel] sober, nice people, and as I can launch into the future, my fancy has more play. Girls write to ask who the little women marry, as if that was the only end and aim of a woman's life. I won't marry Jo to Laurie to please any one."[6]

Louisa focused single-mindedly on writing a novel that reflected an inner vision, and nobody's well-intentioned alternatives dissuaded her. As a result, *Little Women* ranks among the "greats" of enduring classic literature and still delights readers and moviegoers of all ages. Louisa kept her eyes on the goal until she reached it.

Though we're a culture bent on instant gratification, we laud and respect people who dedicate themselves to a creative pursuit, a challenging sport, a business venture, a fit and healthy body. Something within us responds to the act of endurance, the raw determination, of persevering until we win. Yet so few of us do. We love the final result, but we don't embrace the means to obtain the end. We don't stick with it.

Yet achieving anything of value requires single-mindedness—a determination to keep our eyes fixed on the prize until we grasp it. This is as true for soul development as anything else. To shape and grow and deepen the soul, we guard against what neglects spiritual growth and promote what enhances it. We devote noticeable time and energy to the soul's development. We choose to please God rather than people.

We also can check our progress by periodically answering the following questions:

Do I consistently reserve time and energy for soul development? We don't have to slavishly stick to the same schedule, but to grow the soul continually, we need to feed ourselves consistently. Also, it helps to reserve a time when we're still alert and filled with a measure of energy.

Do I infuse variation and creativity into my soulish pursuits? The soul responds heartily to change that replenishes its growth. This means varying our soul-development time, method, location, or other factors, to ward off boredom and predictability. For example, walking and praying could refurbish our intercessions. Listening to soothing music may calm the soul more than our usual reading. Occasionally sharing the time with a friend could sharpen our insights.

Am I steadily progressing toward my soul's growth? Instead of measuring our short-term progress, we look at the overview. We may stumble on the daily route, but overall are we persistently traveling the road to growth? Are we farther along than six months or a year ago?

If we can answer these questions affirmatively, we're keeping our eyes on the goal; we're growing the soul. We can proclaim, "My eyes are ever on the Lord."

Visionary God, keep my heart steadfast and my spiritual eyes focused on you. Teach me your creative ways to grow the soul consistently, to steadily progress toward inner vision.

WITH SWORDS DRAWN
Recognizing Spiritual Warfare

If the LORD had not been on our side
when men attacked us,
when their anger flared against us,
they would have swallowed us alive;
the flood would have engulfed us,
the torrent would have swept over us,
the raging waters
would have swept us away.
Praise be to the LORD,
who has not let us be torn by their teeth.
We have escaped like a bird
out of the fowler's snare;
the snare has been broken,
and we have escaped.

—Psalm 124:2–7

A few weeks before moving away from my hometown to take a job in Christian publishing, a terrible fear paralyzed me with doubts about my career decision. After a Saturday spent wandering around my apartment, dazed and crying, I wanted to back out of this pending transition into ministry.

Toward the day's end, my mother talked to me on the phone and, after listening to my irrational fears, advised, "Judy, you're under spiritual attack. When you attend church tomorrow, ask someone to pray for you. Don't just walk to the altar for help. Run! This is serious business."

The next morning, I stumbled to the altar after a worship service, not sure of who to see or what to say. My pastor stepped forward, I sobbed a few words about fear and ministry, and soon he and the elders circled me and prayed. They didn't just pray for my well-being and for God's will to be done. As the early saints would say, these leaders drew their spiritual swords and "waged warfare" on my behalf. Invoking the name of Jesus, they told the Devil and his evil spirits to flee. They asked Christ to cover me with his blood as a protection from spiritual onslaughts.

Almost as quickly as they'd circled, the elders left, yet I sensed their advance and retreat symbolized the tactical maneuvers of an invisible world. As I remained kneeling, gently crying, an overwhelming peace flooded my soul. Those unseen spirits, circling and taunting me, had fled when believers called on Jesus.

Since then I've experienced other bouts of fear, and sometimes I've mistakenly felt that the problem originated with "just me." I've thought, *If only I could buck up, try harder, be better, I wouldn't feel fearful.* I've had to consistently remind myself that perfect love—God's love—casts out fear, that the Devil enjoys gouging our weak places and pouring terror into them.

When we choose to live from the soul, we're enlisting in spiritual battle. If the enemy can't destroy us, he'll at least try inflicting wounds to bog us down. Circumstances, weaknesses, relationships—he can target any of these for sometimes subtle, sometimes overt warfare of the soul. Consequently, it's crucial to remember that we're engaged in unseen, spiritual battles. Paul reminded us, "For our struggle is not against flesh and blood, but against the rulers, against the authorities, against the powers of this dark world and against the spiritual forces of evil in the heavenly realms."

Like those spiritual leaders at my church, we're to stand firm, with swords drawn, against the soul's invaders. Paul told us how: "Therefore put on the full armor of God, so that when the day of evil comes, you may be able to stand your ground, and after you have done everything, to stand. Stand firm then, with the belt of truth buckled around your waist, with the breastplate of righteousness in place, and with your feet fitted with the readiness that comes from the gospel of peace. In addition to all this, take up the shield of faith, with which you can extinguish all the flaming arrows of the evil one. Take the helmet of salvation and the sword of the Spirit, which is the word of God. And pray in the Spirit on all occasions with all kinds of prayers and requests. With this in mind, be alert and always keep on praying for all the saints."

"I know that for us, it is to be swords drawn, up to the gates of heaven," wrote a young missionary to the suffering Amy Carmichael. "I found great delight in [that] word," she said.[7] We can find delight midst the warfare, too. With swords drawn, we can discover that spiritual fortitude banishes ungodly fear.

Defender of the saints, sharpen my spiritual vision so I can recognize the Devil's attacks. Each day, dress me head-to-toe in the armor of faith and send me out with a sword drawn against the enemy of my soul.

HEAVENLY VIEWS
Anticipating Spiritual Blessings

The LORD remembers us and will bless us:
He will bless the house of Israel,
he will bless the house of Aaron,
he will bless those who fear the LORD—
small and great alike.
May the LORD make you increase,
both you and your children.
May you be blessed by the LORD,
the Maker of heaven and earth.

—Psalm 115:12–15

For the disciple Thomas, seeing was believing. Thomas knew that soldiers had brutally crucified Jesus, and only with his eyes would he believe the Lord breathed again.

"We have seen the Lord!" exclaimed the other disciples, but Thomas replied, "Unless I see the nail marks in his hands, put my finger where the nails were, and put my hand into his side, I will not believe it."

Thomas doubted.

A week later Jesus appeared to the disciples, turned to Thomas, and challenged him, "Put your finger here; see my hands. Reach out your hand and put it into my side. Stop doubting and believe." Thomas cried, "My Lord and my God!"

Thomas believed.

The Lord countered, "Because you have seen me, you have believed; blessed are those who have not seen and yet have believed." Christ was referring to us.

Blessed are we who believe in Jesus Christ, and even more fortunate are we who spiritually see and trust in his promises. To partake in his blessings, God asks us to adopt a heavenly viewpoint that says, "Lord, I believe, even though I see no physical evidence yet." Before receiving the promised blessing, we are blessed already for believing with the eyes of the soul.

To cultivate our spiritual vision, we can pray God's promises as we wait for his blessings. The renowned preacher Peter Marshall modeled "seeing and praying the promises" in a heavenly-minded, faith-filled prayer.

He prayed, "O Lord Jesus, I remember that Thou hast said, 'Lay not up for yourselves treasures upon earth, where moth and rust doth corrupt.' O God, deliver me from falling in love with things. Help me rather to love people, to love principles, to love righteousness, to love Thee.

"Thou hast commanded me 'to seek first the kingdom of God and His righteousness,' and then hast made me a promise that if my heart and mind and soul and will were thus dedicated, I should receive as dividends the very things I see—an abundant ministry unto all my needs.

"O God, help me to believe this. Help me to practice it, that I may find myself that the promise is true, that all my needs shall be met.

"Thou hast invited me 'to ask, to seek, to knock'—assuring me that if I ask, it shall be given unto me; if I seek, I shall find; if I knock, it shall be opened unto me.

"Help me to believe that, O God. Give me the faith to ask, knowing that I shall receive. Give me the faith to seek, believing that I surely shall find. Give me the faith and the persistence to knock, knowing that it shall be indeed opened unto me.

"Help me to live the Christian life in daring faith and humble trust, that there may be worked out in me, even in me, Thy righteousness and goodness. With a sense of adventure, I make this prayer."[8]

With the eyes of the soul we can believe it.

Risen Savior, open my spiritual eyes to see and believe in your promises. I want to be blessed for trusting in your blessings. Give me the faith and persistence to know they shall be opened unto me. Thank you, Lord.

PART NINE

BEING

Placing the Value on Character

Take my life and let it be
Consecrated, Lord, to Thee;
Take my hands, and let them move
At the impulse of Thy love,
At the impulse of Thy love.

Take my feet, and let them be
Swift and beautiful for Thee;
Take my voice, and let me sing
Always, only, for my King,
Always, only, for my King.

Take my moments and my days,
Let them flow in ceaseless praise;
Take my intellect, and use
Ev'ry power as Thou shalt choose,
Ev'ry power as Thou shalt choose.

"TAKE MY LIFE, AND LET IT BE"
BY FRANCES R. HAVERGAL AND CESAR MALAN

My mother fell precariously ill this week, and because we live a thousand miles apart, I feel helpless to comfort her. My sister Barb, who lives next door to Mom, is an excellent caretaker, but I still call Mother twice a day and repeatedly ask God to renew her. Other than that, there isn't much I can do but wait. Healing insists on taking its time.

Mom turns seventy-five next month, and though I pray she'll live for many years, I think about how life will be without her. That image looks so painful I only linger there briefly. Certainly an unfillable chasm will sink into my heart when she dies. No one can replace a mother, especially my mother.

When I ponder Mom's tender relationship with me, I can list lots of memorable activities she's tackled on my behalf: guiding my small hands as we created messy projects in the kitchen; staying up all night to sew a dress for a date; donating articles for my first apartment; shamelessly peddling my books to her friends. Yet despite a long list, what Mom has accomplished isn't what touches me the most; it's who she is. Loving, forbearing, forgiving, understanding, encouraging, persevering. These traits describe my mother. These gifts penetrate my soul, never to be extracted.

Mom's imprint on me stems from her character, and, accordingly, for her daughters she's more concerned about who we are than what we do. Are we kind, honest, giving? Do we try our best and encourage one another? Are we loving wives and mothers, faithful friends? Do we follow God? Scanning my life, I don't recall my mother once asking, "What are you accomplishing?" But I remember many variations on the question, "Who are you being?"

For decades I evaded the "being" question and emphasized the "doing." *Look, Mom, at what I've accomplished. Never mind how I feel about myself or the way I treat others. Marvel at what I've done!*

No doubt Mother felt proud of my accomplishments. She told me so. But her most gratifying moments emerged when I chose actions based on character growth rather than career advancement. That still holds true today.

Mom hopes for me, prays for me, and nurtures me with an expectation that I'll do the same for others. This is her legacy, never to be erased, for it originates with God's desire for every person, every generation without end. It is the way of the soul, the path to true influence and satisfaction.

THE IMPORTANCE OF BEING
Living Outside Secular Boundaries

Blessed are they whose ways are blameless,
who walk according to the law of the LORD.
Blessed are they who keep his statutes
and seek him with all their heart. . . .
Oh, that my ways were steadfast
in obeying your decrees!. . .
I will praise you with an upright heart
as I learn your righteous laws.

—Psalm 119:1–2, 5, 7

The surly Greek philosopher Diogenes disdained materialism and the quest for power. He believed happiness consisted of satisfying a person's basic needs and nothing more.

When Alexander the Great visited Corinth, he found Diogenes living in a large earthenware tub. The king asked, "Diogenes, is there any way I can serve you?"

Preoccupied with sunning himself, Diogenes replied, "Yes, stand out of my sun!"

Alexander's men ridiculed Diogenes, but the king stopped them. "If I were not Alexander," said their ruler, "I should wish to be Diogenes."[1]

Though Alexander possessed everything humans strive for, he respected the simplicity of Diogenes' determination to live outside cultural expectations. Then as now, people extolled power, beauty, prestige, money, admiration, accomplishments, possessions. "Having it all" represented freedom from anyone else's control.

Ironically, gaining these success symbols only tightened the bonds of control. Having it all drew a stifling boundary around Alexander, as it does many of us today. The more we substitute external possessions for internal character, the more we suffocate the life-giving properties of the soul. Piled under with doing and possessing, the soul can't breathe. It withers and nearly dies.

On the other hand, if we loosen society's expectations, daring to live outside secular boundaries, there is hope for resuscitation. If we invert the success formula and elevate "being" over "doing," we live according to God's statutes and the way of everlasting life. We allow the soul to not only survive but thrive. Released from human expectations, we experience real freedom, a spiritual freedom.

"Why, then, is a wise man great? Because he has a great soul," wrote Seneca, the Roman philosopher.[2] Maybe when Alexander the Great encountered Diogenes, the king sensed that true greatness originated from mastering the person within rather than conquering the countries surrounding him. But perhaps when Alexander discovered this, he thought it was too late for alterations.

With matters of the soul, however, it is never too late to change course and revive the person within. Nor does discovering the "importance of being" preclude our doing or owning or succeeding ever again. It does, however, reshuffle our priorities. We put soul work first and everything else after that. In biblical words, we wholeheartedly follow God and seek his kingdom above all else. We become who he wants us to be before doing what he asks us to do. Following God's expectations, we experience real satisfaction, a spiritual satisfaction.

To be or not to be? For the woman who pursues a soul life, that certainly is the question. And the answer is "Take my life, Lord, and *let it be*."

Take my life and let it be consecrated, Lord, to thee. May this old hymn take on new meaning for me, God. Give me the courage to reorganize my priorities so I set aside "doing" and spend time "being." Shape me into who you want me to be. Then with a great and eternally free soul I can do what you would have me to do in the world.

CENTEREDNESS

Learning to Respond from the Soul

LORD, who may dwell in your sanctuary?
Who may live on your holy hill?
He whose walk is blameless
and who does what is righteous,
who speaks the truth from his heart
and has no slander on his tongue,
who does his neighbor no wrong
and casts no slur on his fellowman,
who despises a vile man
but honors those who fear the LORD,
who keeps his oath
even when it hurts. . . .
He who does these things
will never be shaken.

—Psalm 15

It happened once that a group of physicians were in their cups and had fallen into quarreling about which part of the body was most important for life. As they could not agree among themselves, they decided to consult the rabbi.

"'Of course it is the heart and blood vessels that are most important,' said the first physician, 'for on them the whole life of a man depends.'

"'Not at all,' said the second physician. 'It is the brain and nerves which are most vital, for without them, even the heart would not beat.'

"The third physician said, 'You are both wrong. It is the stomach and the digestive passages which are important, for without the proper digestion of food, the body will die.'

"'The lungs are most important,' declared the fourth, 'for a man without air will surely die.'

"'You are all wrong,' said the rabbi. 'There are two vessels of the body only that are important, but you have no knowledge of them.'

"'What are they, then?' asked the physicians.

"The rabbi replied, 'The channel that runs from the ear to the soul, and the one that runs from the soul to the tongue.'"[3]

So far, no doctor has spotted these channels with an X-ray machine, but along with the rabbi, I believe they exist. However, we don't automatically use them to relate to the world. Responding from within to people and events, responding from the soul, takes careful discipline, repeated practice, and extra time.

To respond from within, we listen carefully to what's said and, instead of rattling off a top-of-the-head reaction, we first filter the information through our soul's value system. We ask ourselves, *How does the information or situation settle with God's Spirit within? What are the soul needs of the person confronting us? What would be a wise, loving, spiritually mature response?* Then we respond accordingly.

To be effective, responding from within depends on our continual spiritual development—an emphasis on being who God asks us to be—and a "centeredness" that tunes into the Holy Spirit's impressions on the soul. In effect, we respond from our character—our spiritual, rather than our carnal, nature. Then what "runs from the soul to the tongue" edifies, encourages, and lovingly convicts listeners to find God's heart.

As an added blessing, our tongue's response can also reverberate and replenish us. "My tongue will speak of your righteousness and of your praises all day long," promised David to God. This is the reward of those who respond from well-tended souls.

Tend and cultivate my character, God, so my responses emerge from deep within my soul, where your Spirit dwells within me. Then my tongue will edify and encourage others. Then I'll speak of your righteousness and sing your praises all day long.

PURPOSEFUL PAIN

Forging a Path to Personal Growth

You brought me out of the womb;
you made me trust in you
even at my mother's breast.
From birth I was cast upon you;
from my mother's womb you have been
my God.
Do not be far from me,
for trouble is near
and there is no one to help. . . .
You who fear the LORD, praise him!. . .
For he has not despised or disdained
the suffering of the afflicted one;
he has not hidden his face from him
but has listened to his cry for help.

—Psalm 22:9–11, 23–24

Ellen sat at my dining-room table, a discouraged heap of tears. For weeks she'd prepared an important proposal for her company. A proposal that could pull the business—which for several years had been spiraling downward—

out of the red. Just by looking at her I could tell her presentation hadn't gone well.

Ellen confirmed my assessment with her story. Arriving at the crucial meeting, she had listened and taken notes during two hours of reports from the other department managers, who were all males. The atmosphere felt electric. Then it was Ellen's turn to speak, the last presentation before lunch. As an introduction the president turned to her and smiled wryly, saying, "Now it's time to hear Ellen's little report."

The men had leaned back in their chairs, quipped to each other, and checked their watches as Ellen explained her proposal, feeling deflated.

"I can't believe how a crooked smile and using the word 'little' undermined my credibility," she told me. "The boss let the guys know that my ideas weren't important, but if I confronted him about it, he'd say I'm too sensitive. I'm stuck between a rock and a hard place, and it hurts."

This wasn't the first incident in which Ellen felt discriminated against, nor would it be the last. Nor was Ellen the oversensitive type. In the last year she'd experienced a pileup of pain, and sitting at my table, she awakened to the question, *What am I going to do about it?* For various reasons, Ellen couldn't quit her job anytime soon. She could only do one of two things: let the hard place crush her, or forge a passageway for her soul's freedom.

Whatever pain we experience, traumatic or trivial, we face the same choice. We can get stuck in bitterness and allow the pain to destroy us, or we can use the pain to open a path to inner growth and maturity. We can work toward positive change even when the only option is to let the pain deepen our character and spiritual outlook.

A Jewish survivor of Auschwitz recalled, "It never occurred to me to question God's doings or lack of doings while I was an inmate. . . . I was no less or no more religious because of what the Nazis did to us; and I believe my faith in God was not undermined in the least.

"It never occurred to me to associate the calamity we were experiencing with God, to blame him or believe in him less. . . . God doesn't owe us that, or anything. . . . We owe God our lives for the few or many years we live, and we have the duty to worship him and do as he commands us. That's what we're here on earth for, to be in God's service, to do God's bidding."[4]

This is the admission of a soul committed to purposeful, soulful pain.

All-knowing and ever-loving God, reveal how I can use my pain to forge a path to spiritual growth. I choose to allow the pain to deepen my character and my response to trouble.

HOPE

Living Beyond the Circumstances

I wait for the LORD, my soul waits,
  and in his word I put my hope.
My soul waits for the Lord
  more than watchmen wait for the morning,
  more than watchmen wait for the morning.
O Israel, put your hope in the LORD,
  for with the LORD is unfailing love
  and with him is full redemption.
He himself will redeem Israel
  from all their sins.

—Psalm 130:5–8

A friend pours out her troubles to me and asks, "Should I have hope for this situation? Should I believe God will change things? Or am I in denial?" These days, soul searchers probably ask these questions frequently. We've heard so much about denial and dysfunction, we can confuse them with biblical faith and hope.

I think my friend expresses a true biblical hope, because she's doing her part in the situation but still seeking God as her source for this need. If she were in denial, she'd stick her head in the proverbial sand, do nothing, and still expect God to weave miracles. God is so merciful, he can pull us out of our screwups, but even the "spiritual greats" advise us to work as if everything depends on us and pray as if everything depends on God.[5] When we make a choice, based on God's promises, to abandon ourselves to him and trustingly throw ourselves into difficult circumstances, hope springs forth and grows the soul. In ourselves and in those we encounter.

"Most people want to know if God really makes a difference," explained Rebecca Manley Pippert in *Hope Has Its Reasons.* "Can Jesus help them grow and give meaning and purpose and guidance and strength to their lives too? And when our answer is yes, we have experienced firsthand his power in the midst of pain—we give others hope."[6]

Again, living hopefully, in a biblical sense, traces back to character development—understanding God's desires, and being who he calls us to be. And God asks us to base our being and doing on hope. The hope of his promises, the hope of his return, the hope of heaven. "And hope does not disappoint us, because God has poured out his love into our hearts by the Holy Spirit, whom he has given us."

> We are never beneath hope, while above hell; nor above hope, while beneath heaven.
>
> —ANONYMOUS

> What can be hoped for which is not believed?
>
> —SAINT AUGUSTINE

> When you say a situation or person is hopeless, you are slamming the door in the face of God.
>
> —CHARLES L. ALLEN

> Life with Christ is an endless hope, without him a hopeless end.
>
> —ANONYMOUS

There is more hope for a self-convicted sinner than there is for a self-conceited saint.

—ANONYMOUS

Now faith is being sure of what we hope for and certain of what we do not see.

—THE WRITER OF HEBREWS

God, make me a hope-filled person—someone who instills your hope in others. I want to be filled with your heavenly hope and "sure of what I hope for and certain of what I do not see." God, do not let that hope disappoint me.

LOOSENING UP
Taking Ourselves Less Seriously

O LORD, our Lord,
how majestic is your name in all the earth!
You have set your glory
above the heavens. . . .
When I consider your heavens,
the work of your fingers,
the moon and the stars,
which you have set in place,
what is man that you are mindful of him,
the son of man that you care for him?

—Psalm 8:1, 3–4

In *A Little Book of Forgiveness,* D. Patrick Miller warns that "to carry an anger against anyone is to poison your own heart, administering more toxin every time you replay in your mind the injury done to you."[7] The medical community backs Miller's belief both through doctors' observations and formal research. People who harbor negative emotions succumb more easily to disease than those with inner peace.

Many negative emotions stem from unresolved anger, and medical research links chronic hostility to heart attacks and coronary heart disease, the nation's number-one killer. According to Murray A. Mittleman, M.D., an epidemiologist and Harvard Medical School researcher, the average risk of heart attack more than doubles in the two hours after a moderate or greater outburst of anger. It appears that anger literally lingers in our hearts.

Researchers are also changing doctors' minds about the speed at which we clog artery walls. In the past we've believed that plaques—fat deposits and other materials on the inside of the blood vessel wall—build up slowly and eventually block the heart muscle's blood flow. But new research reveals that sudden elevations in blood pressure can injure or rupture plaques within hours.

"Anger increases the heart rate and blood pressure, which may damage plaques inside the coronary arteries," claims Dr. Mittleman. "The release of adrenaline and other hormones that raise your heart rate and blood pressure also increases the stickiness of your platelets [clotting cells]." This slathers more debris on the artery walls, blocking the blood's flow. To top it off, chronic hostility also assaults the immune system, increasing the risk of infectious diseases.[8]

With so much evidence piling up, experts on anger recommend a homespun remedy. They say, "Loosen up. Let the anger go." It's not an easy prescription to swallow when we're hurting, but it could prolong our lives.

To this advice I'd add, "Don't take yourself so seriously." Often when we're hurt and angry, we're coddling a distorted self-image. We think ourselves more important than we actually are. Or we fear we're not important at all. The Bible reminds us, "Do not think of yourself more highly than you ought, but rather think of yourself with sober judgment, in accordance with the measure of faith God has given you."

Sober judgment lives in between self-inflation and self-degradation. It understands, "The world doesn't revolve around me, but neither am I insignificant."

A soul kept spiritually in tune exercises this sober judgment and seldom wastes time getting angry about things that don't really matter.

When my friend Kathy riles up, she asks herself, "In light of all eternity, what does it matter?" If we ask ourselves the same question, the answer could release our angry mental grip on the rude gas station attendant, the child who embarrasses us, the husband who forgot to stop at the grocery store, the woman who works in a bigger office than ours. We keep the peace within and save our anger for injustices that deserve it.

So when we pursue a biblical spirituality, we can simultaneously work on loosening up. It's not only good for the body, it's life for the soul.

I hand you my anger over the little things, God. I'm loosening up and letting go. Flood me with your peace, the inner calm of a wise soul. Show me how to take myself less seriously.

PART TEN

L O V I N G

Sharing the Soul with Others

Blest be the tie that binds
Our hearts in Christian love;
The fellowship of kindred minds
Is like to that above.

Before our Father's throne
We pour our ardent prayers;
Our fears, our hopes, our aims are one,
Our comforts and our cares.

We share our mutual woes,
Our mutual burdens bear;
And often for each other flows
The sympathetic tear.

When we asunder part
It gives us inward pain;
But we shall still be joined in heart,
And hope to meet again.

"Blest Be the Tie That Binds"
by J. Fawcett and H. G. Nageli

A man with many speaking engagements, Bishop Fulton J. Sheen once was applauded before addressing an interfaith rally in Baltimore.

Raising his hand for silence, the bishop said, "When you applaud me at the start, that's faith. Midway through, that's hope. But, ah, my dear friends, if you applaud me at the end, that will be charity!"[1]

With this jest the bishop touched the pulse of soulful and Christlike relationships. To love one another is to have faith in our strong points, hope for our weaknesses, charity toward our failures. It's knowing when to open and close our eyes so we believe in, and bring out the best in, one another.

Reams of literature and how-to advice exist on love and loving one another, but Paul's instructions have survived the centuries, because they echo God's desire for relationships. "Love is patient, love is kind," Paul wrote. "It does not envy, it does not boast, it is not proud. It is not rude, it is not self-seeking, it is not easily angered, it keeps no record of wrongs. Love does not delight in evil but rejoices with the truth. It always protects, always trusts, always hopes, always perseveres.

"Love never fails."

This is how God loved us.

John, the apostle of love, explained, "This is love: not that we loved God, but that he loved us and sent his Son as an atoning sacrifice for our sins. Dear friends, since God so loved us, we also ought to love one another." Despite our waywardness, God sacrificed his greatest treasure so we could love from redeemed and faithful souls. So we could be soul mates with him and each other.

This is how God still loves us.

"And now these three remain: faith, hope and love. But the greatest of these is love."

VALUABLE DEPENDENCIES

When Need Strengthens the Soul

O God, you are my God,
  earnestly I seek you;
my soul thirsts for you,
  my body longs for you,
in a dry and weary land
  where there is no water....
Because you are my help,
  I sing in the shadow of your wings.
My soul clings to you;
  your right hand upholds me.

—Psalm 63:1, 7–8

On my father's side, I descend from a family of feisty siblings. The Couchman family folklore fills with remembrances of fistfights among teenage brothers, intensely loyal sisters, and a strong-willed mother presiding over them all. At the same time, Dad's siblings have been giving, close-knit, hard-working, and loving, especially toward their children and grandchildren. I'm a fortunate recipient of that fierce love, but I've also inherited the ability to harbor resentment.

A poignant case of family conflict occurred between an aunt and uncle, my father's sister and brother. Today no one remembers exactly why, but these two didn't speak to each other for about thirty years even though they lived in the same city. As best I can decipher, my uncle fell and hit his head in a work-related accident. My aunt suggested he visit the Mayo Clinic for some residual physical problems, and when my uncle refused, they exchanged harsh words, and a stony silence wedged between them. In a quizzical twist, a love gesture constructed the foundation for a burgeoning wall of resentment.

Then, after decades of silence, my uncle's wife died suddenly. Immediately my uncle called his sister, and she rushed to his side. They've stayed in touch ever since.

I wonder if deep inside, this aunt and uncle wanted to forgive each other, but it took an acute personal crisis—something that finally broke spirits—to acknowledge their eternal connectedness and need for one another. I'll probably never know for sure, but most likely something had eroded inside of them, something they hoped forgiveness would repair. It's wonderful to hear about them now, though. They're a relationship on the mend. They're learning to trust and depend on each other again, to need each other. For this I love them more than ever before.

Perhaps because I share their genes, maybe because I'm a baby boomer, or simply because I'm a sinner, I've been a feisty, independent type too. In young adulthood I thought needing and depending on others constituted weakness. I cast out on my own, moved away from family, lived by myself, tried making my mark on the world. I acquired success and failure, age and experience, foes and friendships. And here's what I learned: people need each other.

More specifically, I need people—family, friends, networks, mentors, neighbors, the friendly clerk at the grocery store. I need people who'll dig into my life and laugh, advise, applaud, caution, encourage, question, commiserate, and smile into my face and say I look fine. And yes, people who will forgive me after years of detachment.

Ongoing, loving relationships fill something within us that nothing else can; they provide spiritual connection and strengthen the inner person. We're not meant to manage life on our own, at least not without strangling the soul. God created us for relationships, and this desire pulsates within because it models our need for God.

Viewed from this vantage point, needing people is the beginning of strength and wisdom and fulfillment. Even if we're feisty and strong-willed. Especially when we long to please God.

Lord, you are the giver of relationships, and I need what you give to me through people. I lay down my independent spirit and offer up empty hands to grasp the hands of others. Teach me the humility to say, "I need you" and grow strong in my soul because of that need.

TIME TO WASTE
Throwing Away a Valuable Commodity

May God be gracious to us and bless us
  and make his face shine upon us,
that your ways may be known on earth,
  your salvation among all nations.
May the peoples praise you, O God;
  may all the peoples praise you.
May the nations be glad and sing for joy,
  for you rule the peoples justly
  and guide the nations of the earth. . . .
God will bless us,
  and all the ends of the earth will fear him.

—Psalm 67:1–4, 7

My friend Susan calls and says she's on her way to Starbucks for coffee. Will I join her?

"No, no," I say. "I'm still in my robe. It'd take too much time to get ready and get together. This morning I need to write."

As I hang up the phone, I think, *It would have been nice to go. My work-at-home schedule is flexible. Why is it so hard for me to say yes?* For some reason, I think it's more virtuous to stick with my work than to spend an hour with a friend. An inner voice says I'd be wasting time, but do these words speak the truth?

I don't believe that time spent cultivating a relationship, those moments or hours passed with meaningful people, is wasted. Especially not time with someone as interesting and vital to me as Susan. Especially not when I spend day after day alone to write.

So what really stops me from hovering together over coffee?

I turn from the telephone and pull out the morning's work.

Two hours later I take stock: Have I written as fluently as I intended? Hardly. My creativity hasn't moved much for two days. Ideas and sentences eke out like hardened molasses. In my mind, though, a puritanical voice recites advice dispensed to authors: *Write every day. Write no matter how you feel. Write, write, write!*

Wrong, wrong, wrong, I answer back, startling myself. I've reached the law of diminishing returns. I need human contact. I need to drink coffee with Susan. To prove this to myself, I mentally review what experience has taught me but I too easily forget.

When I "waste" valuable time with Susan—if I hang out at her favorite coffee shop and listen to her life—I express my love. I show she's more valuable than a manuscript. I touch her soul and she reaches into mine. "Throwing away" time with Susan expresses love to myself too. Being together refreshes my brain, reignites my creativity, and reaffirms who I am in the world. I return to my work recharged.

So I ask myself again, *What stops me from buying that cup of coffee?*

The answer is neither poetic nor sensible, as I would hope.

The answer is that I've developed a bad habit.

I'm in the habit of saying no, thinking it more efficient to work and "not waste my time." But for the sake of my soul and its relationships, I need to develop the habit of "wasting time" on people, of throwing away a precious commodity to love them as Christ does, of refilling my cup when I'm empty.

Ancient wisdom tells us, "Cast your bread upon the waters, for after many days you will find it again." Another rendition of the same principle is, "Give, and it will be given to you. A good measure, pressed down, shaken together and running over, will be poured into your lap. For with the measure you use, it will be measured to you."

Starbucks is still open. I'm going to call Susan.

Loving and giving God, thank you for "wasting your time" on me—for giving everything so I can live from a redeemed soul. Based on your example, I want to "waste time" on others, loving them beyond the obligations in my life.

OPENING UP
Daring to Speak the Truth

Then I said, "Here I am, I have come—
    it is written about me in the scroll.
I desire to do your will, O my God;
    your law is within my heart."
I proclaim righteousness in the great assembly;
    I do not seal my lips,
    as you know, O LORD.
I do not hide your righteousness in my heart;
    I speak of your faithfulness and salvation.
I do not conceal your love and your truth
    from the great assembly.

—Psalm 40:7–10

I shifted in the morning breeze, focusing more on my unflattering dress than on the wedding ceremony. Several months earlier I'd threatened to boycott this event if our bridesmaid dresses were pink, sleeveless, printed with large flowers, or tight at the waist. Now I stood at Michelle's outdoor nuptials, flapping in the wind, wearing all of the above.

I found this hard to believe, but not as difficult as realizing this was Michelle's wedding—or at least that she'd chosen to marry Ron, a worse match than me and a flowery dress. Aside from personality clashes, the bride and groom differed in faith. Michelle followed Christ; Ron did not.

As Michelle walked the garden path toward Ron and the minister, I imagined grabbing her, veil and all, and racing across the park toward safety. Away from her big mistake, away from the confusion, away from exposing my thick arms to wedding guests. But it was too late to protest Michelle's choice—in bridesmaid dresses or a marriage partner. As the bridal party turned toward the minister, I wanted to erase the future. In a few hours I could banish this dress, but Michelle's commitment to Ron was for a lifetime.

During the reception, I retreated to a corner table, finally away from the arm-inspecting crowd but not far from misgivings about this new marriage. Soon another attendant positioned herself across the table, looked around, and asked, "Well, how do you feel about the wedding?"

I sighed and cleared my throat.

"Not so hot, huh? I feel the same way," she whispered. "Actually, I don't think Ron's a Christian. I'm surprised she married him. Michelle's such a strong believer."

With that admission, my throat unlocked and doubts tumbled out. Together we worried and wondered. Would this marriage last? Should we have confronted Michelle about her choice? We felt guilty about our silence and partly responsible for this wrong decision. What could we do now? Nothing except vow to speak up when other friends headed toward spiritual disaster, marital or otherwise.

As we feared, different values have battered Ron and Michelle's marriage, and through the years I've chastised myself for stifling those premarital concerns. Despite this couple's difficulties, though, it's still hard to confront a friend or family member about a hazardous choice or sinful relationship.

Why? Because I can confuse unconditional love with acceptance of sin, plus I dislike risking their rejection of me and our relationship. I want to love these people as Jesus does—freely, deeply, eternally—but I forget that he spoke out against sin and its devastations. He risked everything—his reputation, relationships, and life—to speak God's truth to the righteous and unrighteous alike.

Slowly, ever so slowly I'm learning that to save someone's soul, speaking the truth can be the most loving thing to do.

Loving Father, I need your discernment about when to speak up and when to remain silent. When I am to speak out, teach me to present the truth in love. Help the people I confront to hear the love in my voice and consider your redemption.

THE SEARCH FOR INTIMACY
Creating a Safe Place to Be

I rejoiced with those who said to me,
"Let us go to the house of the LORD."
Our feet are standing
in your gates, O Jerusalem. . . .
Pray for the peace of Jerusalem:
"May those who love you be secure.
May there be peace within your walls
and security within your citadels."
For the sake of my brothers and friends,
I will say, "Peace be within you."

—Psalm 122:1–2, 6–8

During lunch with a Christian colleague, I mentioned how being spiritually discipled by an older woman helped me understand God better.

She stiffened and raised her voice, "Don't use language like that!"

With a French fry lodged in my throat, I looked around for anyone who might have heard her. "What language?" I whispered.

"'Discipling!' You want to help businesswomen know Christ? Then learn how to talk to them! They don't know what discipling means, or if they do, they think it's repressive. Businesspeople are into mentoring!"

She continued with a tirade about religious lingo and Stone Age Christians. I don't remember much after that except that I wanted to crawl out of the restaurant. I'd only wanted to talk about my growing relationship with God. I never brought up the topic again.

To engage in conversation that feeds the soul, it's crucial to create a safe and confidential place to be ourselves, to honestly express what we think and feel. And to listen.

"In the practice of friendship, we might keep this important aspect of soul in mind: its need for containment," says therapist Thomas Moore in *Soul Mates*. "A friend could offer containment by receiving another's feelings and thoughts without a strong need for interpretation or commentary. Sometimes, of course, we ask friends to offer their opinions and judgments, but even then we expect a high degree of acceptance and recognition of who we are. In friendship, we want to receive and be received."[2]

To learn to receive someone in conversation, to create a protected place of intimacy, we can evaluate our listening techniques with these questions (if we're listening from the soul, the answers will be yes):

Do I listen as much as I talk?
Do I focus on what the person is saying rather than what I'll say next?
Do I not allow personal biases to block listening or responding?
Do I not interrupt the person's explanations?
Do I allow my friend to be honest rather than expect a specific response?
Do I respond instead of react?
Do I think before I respond?
Do I respond in love even if I don't agree?
If appropriate, do I keep the conversation confidential even if I'm not asked to?

As we talk, we probably won't listen perfectly, but if we keep these principles in mind, we'll increasingly engage in sacred exchanges. We'll receive an individual's soul and be invited to give ours in return—and hopefully, when the person peers inside us, he or she will meet the Christ within.

A stirring line in the musical *Les Misérables* proclaims, "To love another person is to see the face of God."[3] So it is when we listen and give each other our souls.

Listening Father, I want to receive and thoughtfully respond to other people's souls. Let them say, "To be loved and listened to by her is to see the face of God."

ENDURING LOVE
Giving Up on Comparisons

Surely God is good to Israel,
  to those who are pure in heart.
But as for me, my feet had almost slipped;
  I had nearly lost my foothold.
For I envied the arrogant
  when I saw the prosperity of the wicked. . . .
When I tried to understand all this,
  it was oppressive to me
till I entered the sanctuary of God;
  then I understood their final destiny.

—Psalm 73:1–3, 16–17

Once upon a time a hungry, thirsty fox stole into a vineyard and eyed some sun-ripened grapes on a trellis. "I'd give anything to have those grapes," he said with a watering mouth, but the grapes hung beyond the fox's reach.

Still desiring the grapes, the fox ran and jumped, snapping at the nearest bunch. He missed. Again and again he leaped, falling short of the grapes each time. Finally, exhausted and bitter, the fox crawled away from the trellis.

"Well, I never really wanted those grapes. They were probably sour and wormy anyway," he complained. The moral: Any fool can despise what he cannot get.[4]

Aesop told this story generations ago, but the moral still applies today. When we want something we can't obtain, life turns into sour grapes, especially when somebody else has what we're striving for. Many of us pass through times when we ask, "Why is her life better than mine?" or "Why does she get what I'm longing to have? She's not better than me!" This question particularly stings when the other person doesn't follow God or blatantly lives wickedly.

While we're on earth, these questions elicit no definitive answer, but they do point to what's rumbling inside us. When we want something that belongs to someone else, we're coveting. God felt so strongly about this sin that it's included in the Ten Commandments. He declared, "You shall not covet your neighbor's house. You shall not covet your neighbor's wife, or his manservant or maidservant, his ox or donkey, or anything that belongs to your neighbor."

Roughly translated, coveting anything that belongs to anyone else is sin. It poisons the heart and kills the soul's relationships.

Since humanity began, we've struggled to possess what we don't have. Nations fight for disputed land, children battle over toys, coworkers resent the person who got promoted. From the petty to the earth-shattering, it's difficult to stay content with what we have—and not to resent those with more than us. Unless arrested by God's Spirit, possessiveness grows into an insatiable desire.

"Mankind . . . esteem that which they have most desired as of no value the moment it is possessed, and torment themselves with fruitless wishes for that which is beyond their reach," wrote archbishop Fénélon. He cited the cause as "the perverse depravity of their nature."[5]

With our sophisticated mind-set, it's uncomfortable to think of ourselves as "perverse" and "depraved." But if we truly believe God's Word, those descriptions fit our innermost hearts. Scripture says, "All have turned aside, they have together become corrupt; there is no one who does good, not even one." Yet once again, if we believe God's promises, he will forgive us our sins and cleanse us from unrighteousness. He will forgive our pettiness, comparisons, and covetousness. He will free the soul to love despite the inequalities.

Dear Creator and Giver of all things, I don't always understand how you distribute your gifts to your children. I particularly don't understand why my friend is prospering while I'm struggling. Instead of insisting on "evening the score," I ask that you forgive my sin of covetousness, releasing me to love and rejoice with her.

HOLY LOVE
Loving the Unlovable

Blessed is he who has regard for the weak;
  the LORD delivers him in times of trouble....
Even my close friend, whom I trusted,
  he who shared my bread,
  has lifted up his heel against me.
But you, O LORD, have mercy on me;
  raise me up, that I may repay them.
I know that you are pleased with me,
  for my enemy does not triumph over me.
In my integrity you uphold me
  and set me in your presence forever.

—Psalm 41:1, 9–12

I needed some physical exercise that evening, so I took up channel surfing with the television's remote control. *Boring. Dumb sitcom. Seen that already,* I thought as the programs flicked by. *Why am I wasting my time?*

Then I hit on it: a Christian station featuring a stocky preacher lathered up about quite a few unrelated things. I watched for a few moments, then squinted. *Could it be?* While pounding away about the evils of homosexuality, he smirked and offered a limp-wristed mimic of a gay man. Then with no pause the preacher shifted to women. He spewed out the words so fast, I didn't catch them verbatim, but the gist of the pummeling said, "When we let women make decisions, they'll just use their intuition, and that can lead to all kinds of trouble, like witchcraft."

I clicked off the television, an unconscious reflex probably due to the shock. For a moment my mind blanked out, and then it snapped back. *What? He really believes that?*

By the time I switched on the channel again, the preacher had shuttled to less offensive opinions. I punched the remote and sat staring at the blank screen, incredulous and angry. *How in the world did he get on television? This is the type of condemning rhetoric that makes people turn away from God and the church. Plus, as a woman, this insults me!*

If the person uttering this prejudice against women had been a nonbeliever, I could have chalked up his comments to the darkened spirit within him. I could have pontificated about "loving the unlovely" who don't know God. But this was different. This man, an ordained minister, was a spiritual brother. Jesus said I'm to love my spiritual family, but the preacher was spiteful, ignorant, and embarrassing. Love him? He should know better!

Twenty years ago John White wrote *The Fight,* a book for new Christians. Early on he confronted imperfection in the spiritual family, and for two decades I've repeatedly returned to his wisdom: "You will discover that some Christians are stupid, ornery, tactless, 'stuffed shirts,' prudes, hypocrites and so on. Remember that God loves them even though you find it hard to. You must be charitable enough to admit that there may be unattractive features in your own personality. You don't wear robes and sandals yourself! You must realize that the same new life that is in you is in them. Look well at their faults and see for yourself that the miracle of a new life does not guarantee beauty of character. The life needs to grow and develop."[6]

I could argue that the minister has wasted years of opportunity to improve his character, but, searching the Scriptures, I find Jesus offering the same solution to his followers again and again. He says to love our brothers and love our oppressors, even if brothers and oppressors are the same people. He doesn't say to condone or enable or placate sin, but still to love the sinners. We're to love those who revile us, persecute us, and act as though we don't own brains. We're to love the unlovable no matter who they are.

We love them so we can live above revenge and bitterness and accomplish, unencumbered, God's purposes on the earth. We love them to become more like Christ. We love so the Holy Spirit can heal our hearts of their abuse. So we can dialogue and live together as one. So we can walk the jagged edge of relentless love.

Again and again, for the sake of my soul, I've asked the Lord, "Without you, I can't love this person. Please show me how."

God, there are some people I don't even remotely want to love. Create a miracle in my heart so I can. Teach me to not only say I love them but, by my actions, show them love.

PART ELEVEN

SERVING

Doing What Grows the Soul

Use me today, O Saviour divine!
Cleanse and renew this servant of Thine.
Lord, with Thy Spirit fill me, I pray,
Then, in Thy service, use me today.

Use me today, Lord, use even me,
Use me to lead some lost one to Thee;
Lead me where Thou wilt, Lord, open the way,
And to Thy glory, use me today.

Use me today to scatter the seed,
Bringing the blessing someone may need.
Whether I toil or quietly pray,
Blessed Lord Jesus, use me today.

"USE ME TODAY"
BY GERTRUDE R. DUGAN AND GEORGE C. STEBBINS

A pile of trendy books about soul development sits precariously on my desk. I've just rifled through them, looking for information on serving others from the soul.

In these books, that advice doesn't exist. I find plenty about nurturing the soul, developing soul mates, revitalizing spirituality, taking in solitude, but there is nothing about service, about giving out from the soul. All of the information centers on nurturing ourselves as an end rather than as a means to an end. It's all about making ourselves feel, if not good, at least better.

This is the danger of soul development. After finally convincing ourselves to quiet down and spend time with God, we can forget to rise up again and spill our soul's fullness on others. We're tempted to lavish soul growth on ourselves, ignoring Christ's example of following solitude with times of service and sacrifice.

Taking in is only half of the soul-development cycle. Aside from being receivers of God's words, we're to be givers of those words. We're to be spiritual doers as well as hearers. Otherwise we're headed toward the soul's implosion. If we're all knowledge and no action, something inside eventually bursts and exposes us as spiritual frauds.

James admonished the early Christians, "Do not merely listen to the word, and so deceive yourselves. Do what it says. Anyone who listens to the word but does not do what it says is like a man who looks at his face in a mirror and, after looking at himself, goes away and immediately forgets what he looks like. But the man who looks intently into the perfect law that gives freedom, and continues to do this, not forgetting what he has heard, but doing it—he will be blessed in what he does."

In the days ahead, as we evolve from merely hearing into actively doing, we can remember this poetic truth from an unknown author:

> No service in itself is small,
> None great though earth it fill;
> But that is small that seeks its own,
> And great that seeks God's will.[1]

TAKING IN
A Time for Self-Nourishment

In you, O LORD, I have taken refuge;
  let me never be put to shame;
  deliver me in your righteousness.
Turn your ear to me,
  come quickly to my rescue;
be my rock of refuge,
  a strong fortress to save me.
Since you are my rock and my fortress,
  for the sake of your name lead and guide me.

—Psalm 31:1–3

It was New Year's Day and Roger faced a decision. Should he stay home and watch the football game (which he really wanted to do) or accept an invitation to his friend's house? If Roger visited his friend Chuck, he was in for an afternoon of Bible study. Not quite the typical holiday fare.

"Roger," Chuck had said, "I've a taped sermon that I'd like for you to hear. It's helped me spiritually, and it might help you too." Roger accepted the unusual holiday invitation, but not without reluctance.

That invitation, that sermon, revolutionized Roger's soul life.

For an hour Roger listened to a tape that taught basic principles about spiritual nourishment, but he took notes as though his life depended on it.

"Actually, my life *did* depend on it, because the speaker outlined a format for creating consistent and meaningful time with God," recalled Roger. "Although I'd been a Christian for several years, I struggled with spending time alone with God, and my lack of discipline bothered me. But after hearing that sermon, it changed."

Using a journal, Roger began reading Scripture every day and recording his responses to it according to these categories: (1) a new thought about God, Jesus, the Holy Spirit, or Satan; (2) a sin to avoid; (3) a command to obey; (4) a blessing to enjoy; (5) a promise to claim.

"Thanks to that sermon, I've taught this method to other believers, and now, twenty years later, boxes of journals chronicle my spiritual journey," said Roger. "Someday I want my grandchildren to read those journals, to understand what I stood for and to feel encouraged by the Lord's guidance in my life and theirs."

For the many years I've known them, Roger and his wife, Kathy, have—in addition to their daytime jobs—served their spiritual family, helping Christians grow closer to God. This service can be simultaneously rewarding and disappointing, so individually and together they practice self-nourishment to keep spiritually strong and attuned. I can't think of anyone else as consistent as they are about practicing spiritual disciplines, and it shows in their character; they are people to learn from.

Roger and Kathy differ in personality from me, so my artistic nature chafes at their structured methods. What I want to emulate, though, is their consistency. If I'm not regularly taking in the spiritual, I've nothing spiritual to give while serving others.

I believe this is true for anyone living from the soul. The intake method doesn't matter as much as the consistency. Consistent intake affects who we are, and if we're feeding from God, we'll serve and influence others with Spirit-swept souls.

"Of all commentaries upon the Scriptures, good examples are the best and the liveliest," commented the preacher and poet John Donne in a wedding sermon.[2] His insight is good motivation to keep our souls wedded to heaven while serving on earth.

Holy Spirit, woo me to you. Keep me feeding on the spiritual so I can consistently and significantly serve others. I want a soul wedded to heaven but a life that makes a difference on earth.

INSISTING ON MEANING
Offering Each Day as a Sacrament

> Teach us to number our days aright,
>   that we may gain a heart of wisdom. . . .
> Satisfy us in the morning with your unfailing love,
>   that we may sing for joy and be glad all our
>   days. . . .
> May your deeds be shown to your servants,
>   your splendor to their children.
> May the favor of the Lord our God rest upon us;
>   establish the work of our hands for us—
>   yes, establish the work of our hands.
>
> —Psalm 90:12, 14, 16–17

One of the greatest examples of twentieth-century servanthood resides in Mother Teresa, a Catholic nun serving in India. Since 1948 she's served the poor by "providing a presence of love" in a run-down neighborhood of Calcutta.

Mother Teresa finds meaning in service by seeing Christ in each face she encounters. To cultivate this "way of seeing," she balances a life of action with contemplation. "These two aspects of life, action and contemplation, instead of excluding each other, call for each other's help, implement and complete each other," she explains.

"The latter, when it gets to a certain degree of intensity, diffuses some of its excess on the first. By contemplation the soul draws directly from the heart of God the graces which the active life must distribute."

The word "contemplation" can scare away our modern hearts; we fear it requires more time and mysticism than we can muster. We know that time away to renew is important, but most of us can't manage musing with God as frequently as those in a convent. However, we can practice an "active contemplation" by daily looking for Christ in the faces we encounter. We can offer each day as a sacrament by infusing spiritual meaning into our work.

Mother Teresa says, "I think if we can spread this prayer, if we can translate it into our lives, it will make all the difference."

Dear Jesus,
Help us to spread your fragrance everywhere we go.
Flood our souls with your Spirit and life.
Penetrate and possess our whole being so utterly
that our lives may only be a radiance of yours.
Shine through us
and be so in us
that every soul we come in contact with
may feel your presence in our soul.
Let them look up and see no longer us
but only Jesus.
Stay with us
and then we shall begin to shine as you shine,
so to shine as to be light to others.
The light, O Jesus, will be all from you.
None of it will be ours.
It will be shining on others through us.
Let us thus praise you in the way you love best
by shining on those around us.
Let us preach you without preaching,

not by words, but by our example,
by the catching force,
the sympathetic influence of what we do,
the evident fullness of the love our hearts bear to you.[3]

Lord, let me praise you by shining your love on those around me. Let me preach you without preaching. Help me spread your fragrance everywhere, offering each day as a sacrament.

GOD'S FOOL

Moving Out of the Comfort Zone

You are not a God who takes pleasure in evil;
 with you the wicked cannot dwell. . . .
But I, by your great mercy,
 will come into your house;
in reverence will I bow down
 toward your holy temple.
Lead me, O LORD, in your righteousness
 because of my enemies—
 make straight your way before me.

—Psalm 5:4, 7–8

A friend of mine is dying to get me to sleep in a tent. Not just any tent. It's got to be pitched in the Colorado mountains, surrounded by prickly trees and cooties that bite in the night. No mirrors. No running water and certainly no appliances.

Ana focuses on this goal because she knows that my idea of "roughing it" is forfeiting room service or pillow mints and preferably not both. So when she plies me with phrases like "getting out of your comfort zone" and insists that "everyone else around here likes camping and hiking," I change the subject.

I'm concerned, however, that my defense tactics won't last for long. Sometimes late at night I wonder if there's a groundswell of friends plotting to cast me into a secluded campsite where I can't shave my legs or armpits for at least a week. Just the thought can rob me of a good night's sleep. (Agony, thy name is camping!)

On a deeper level, though, my anticamping stance probably perplexes some friends. They consider me a risk taker, the unusual-idea person, the one who will go nuts if I'm not searching for the next creative challenge. They look at my résumé and professional accomplishments and think I'd be up for most anything. So it could surprise some folks that I admit that sometimes I'm *really scared*.

The truth is, most new experiences rattle my security, and I work hard to camouflage my misgivings. Though I sometimes fool others, I can't hide the fear from myself. So when Ana talks about camping, she unwittingly unsettles a fear submerged inside me. An overnighter in the great outdoors would careen me out of my comfort zone, maybe even make me look foolish. And I hate that more than I loathe bugs and sweat.

It sounds silly, but this camping threat forces me to realize that yes, I take risks, but I dive into situations where I know the territory and feel destined to succeed. These days, however, I'm uncomfortable with being so comfortable, and I can't imagine how I'm grieving God. He sent Jesus to proclaim, "The Spirit of the Sovereign LORD is on me, because the LORD has anointed me to preach good news to the poor. He has sent me to bind up the brokenhearted, to proclaim freedom for the captives and release from darkness for the prisoners, to proclaim the year of the LORD's favor and the day of vengeance of our God, to comfort all who mourn, and provide for those who grieve in Zion—to bestow on them a crown of beauty instead of ashes, the oil of gladness instead of mourning, and a garment of praise instead of a spirit of despair."

That sounds like out of the comfort zone to me—and spiritually convicting—so I'm searching to serve in ways that push my safe limits. I want to be uncomfortable for God. I'm squeamish setting this goal, but I'm comforted that uncomfortable service pleases him.

Are you willing to get uncomfortable, too?

Lord Jesus, I want to get uncomfortable for you. Open a pathway for me to bind up the brokenhearted and comfort those who mourn. Praying this request makes me uncomfortable, so I need your peace. As I cast out in service, I anticipate your joy.

GUIDING

Helping Others Live Soulfully

Since you are my rock and my fortress,
  for the sake of your name lead and guide me.
Free me from the trap that is set for me,
  for you are my refuge.
Into your hands I commit my spirit;
  redeem me, O LORD, the God of truth.
I hate those who cling to worthless idols;
  I trust in the LORD.

—Psalm 31:3–6

In the Old Testament, Laban, the wealthy sheep breeder, misused his role as a family's leader. Instead of valuing his position as a place of service and guidance, he used it for personal gain. Laban profited from his sister Rebekah's marriage to Isaac and used his daughters, Rachel and Leah, as bargaining chips to trick his son-in-law Jacob and benefit financially.

Over time, Jacob outwitted his father-in-law, but Laban still couldn't admit his selfishness and fought for control by requesting that his son-in-law leave Haran. The upshot is that God's will won in the end, and Laban's story stands eternally as an example of how *not* to guide groups or individuals.

If we desire to guide people in their soul lives, it's eye-opening to study the Gospels, learning from, and modeling our path after, Christ's route to influence. Jesus *served* the people and told his followers, "Let ... him who is the chief and leader [become] as one who serves." When we realize we're serving rather than ordering others about, we tap into a personally humbling but spiritually powerful dimension of guidance. We begin empowering people with Christ's Spirit.

"Empowerment" is a current buzzword that makes some Christians uneasy because certain people teach it as a means of self-gratification. But when placed in the context of soul guidance, it describes a biblical goal. To empower people is to equip them to be effective. Christ prepared the disciples for life without him; Paul instructed Timothy how to live as a Christian and a spiritual leader.

Instead of creating dependency, soul guidance empowers people to learn, grow, think for themselves, and discover their own solutions within biblical parameters. To empower means to prompt instead of control, to applaud the desired end result instead of nit-picking at the process, to care about people's growth and maturity instead of our reputation, to abolish legalistic or politically motivated relationships.

Speaking to a Harvard graduating class, Alexandr Solzhenitsyn explained this about legalistic, nonempowering relationships: "A society [or group] based on the letter of the law and never reaching any higher, fails to take advantage of the full range of human possibilities. The letter of the law is too cold and formal to have a beneficial influence. ... Whenever the tissue of life is woven of legalistic relationships, this creates an atmosphere of spiritual mediocrity that paralyzes men's noblest impulses."[4]

True soul guidance, true servanthood, pulls spiritual wanderers out of their mediocrity and into God's light. And where the Spirit and light of God dwells, there is vibrant, powerful, penetrating life that only he can contain.

God, you are light- and life-giving. Penetrate me so your life spills out to others, guiding them to spiritual fullness, greatness, and influence. Teach me to prompt instead of control, to applaud the desired end result instead of nitpicking at the process, to care about people's growth and maturity instead of my reputation, to abolish my legalistic or political motivations. Empower me to empower others.

SPENDING YOURSELF

Serving Without Reservation

Praise the LORD, O my soul;
all my inmost being, praise his holy name.
Praise the LORD, O my soul,
and forget not all his benefits—
who forgives all your sins
and heals all your diseases,
who redeems your life from the pit
and crowns you with love and compassion,
who satisfies your desires with good things
so that your youth is renewed like the eagle's.

—Psalm 103:1–5

Recently I spent a weekend with the Summit Group, a network of female lay leaders who guide ministries for professional and businesswomen. Out of thirty participants only two worked as ministry professionals. The rest juggle full-time jobs, families, and their growing outreaches to women.

As I listened to these visionaries dialogue in groups and talk over meals, a recurring theme intrigued me: Women today create so many personal boundaries, they don't know how to "spend themselves" for God. They labor hard at jobs, turning into workaholics and burnout victims, but they know little about the soul-purifying business of giving a cup of water in Jesus' name.

To their credit, the Summit leaders offered this insight as a loving concern rather than a gripe. They desire that women, whatever their circumstances, grow in God—and spiritual service contributes to the soul's development.

Spending ourselves for God differs from working ourselves to death. Workaholism and burnout result from doing too much, doing it with our limited resources, doing things to please ourselves. Spending ourselves for God involves doing only what God asks of us, doing it through his supernatural power, doing things to meet the needs of others. Spending ourselves for God, serving for and through him without reservation revitalizes the inner person rather than destroys her. Worn and weary at the day's end, the soul feels full of God's pleasure, not empty from self-gratification.

We can spend ourselves for God through our jobs, our families, our friendships, our ministries. The locations and methods vary, but the soul's attitude stays fixed on spiritual service. With this in mind, Brother Roger, founder of a French community dedicated to reconciliation, asks, "Are you going to let yourself fall asleep in dull indifference? Will your lips and your heart become frozen in an attitude of 'what's the use, we can't do anything, let things take their course?' Will you let yourself sink into discouragement like Elijah, that believer of times gone by, who, convinced that he could do nothing more for his people, collapsed under a tree to fall asleep and forget?

"Or will you remain awake and take your place among those women, men and children who have decided to act? Through a life of inner peace, sharing and solidarity, they speak to us, they help us go forward. They possess unexpected energies in order to take on responsibilities. They know that faith enables us to resist the worst torments, the soul overflowing with hope and love."[5]

Will we decide to act? With full souls, will we spend ourselves?

We answer not just by saying yes but by our commitment to active service.

Jesus, you set the perfect example of spending yourself for God.
With my imperfections, I commit to spending myself for you.
Show me what to do.

PART TWELVE

CELEBRATING

Rejoicing in Each Day

Praise Him! praise Him! Jesus, our blessed Redeemer!
Sing, O earth—His wonderful love proclaim!
Hail Him! hail Him! highest archangels in glory;
Strength and honor give to His holy name!

Like a shepherd Jesus will guard His children,
In His arms He carries them all day long;
Praise Him! praise Him! tell of His excellent greatness,
Praise Him! praise Him! ever in joyful song.

Praise Him! praise Him! Jesus, our blessed Redeemer!
Heav'nly portals loud with hosannas ring!
Jesus, Saviour, reigneth forever and ever;
Crown Him! crown Him! Prophet, and Priest, and
King!

Christ is coming! over the world victorious,
Pow'r and glory unto the Lord belong;
Praise Him! praise Him! tell of His excellent greatness,
Praise Him! praise Him! ever in joyful song.

"PRAISE HIM! PRAISE HIM!"
BY FANNY J. CROSBY AND CHESTER G. ALLEN

A friend of Luci Swindoll calls her "the most alive and celebratory person I know."

In her book *Celebrating Life,* Luci described her cause for celebration. She wrote, "I hadn't been on this earth very many years when it began to sink in that lots of things were not going to go my way. I'd get all excited about a plan or an event that was on the horizon of my life, when suddenly things didn't pan out and my spirit would hit rock bottom with a mighty thud.

"There was always a thief waiting in the wings to steal my joy and enthusiasm. I hated that. So much so that it struck me (sort of like being run over by a large truck), 'How long are you going to live like this? How long are you going to let life sit on top of you with its disappointments, anxieties, pressures, and regrets? Why don't you figure out a way to beat life at its own game?'

"That's when I decided to begin dwelling on the positive instead of the negative. That's when celebrating life became a conscious choice, a decision to live fully, every day and in every way, to the degree I was able. That's when I realized that the presence of God could actually enter into my circumstances and change things for the better. And, oh, what a difference that change in attitude has made in the way I face life!

"Believe it or not, we all have many reasons to celebrate life in spite of the situations in which we find ourselves. Today. This minute. There is something—some perk—in your life that is cause for celebration. Think about it. Start this way: Look at the hour before you, with its myriad demands, plans, concerns, and problems and ask God, in the midst of all that, to give you a perk, just for the love of life . . . no other reason.

"We all lead such busy, stressful lives. We feel overwhelmed. We experience pressure and nagging deadlines that drive us crazy. To celebrate anything for any reason would never enter our thinking. But believe me, we need those perks to keep going. They sweeten the bitter tastes of life.

"The highest and most desirable state of the soul is to praise God in celebration for being alive. Without perks our lives are easily lost in the world of money, machines, anxieties or inertia. Our poor, splendid souls! How they fight for food! They have forgotten how to celebrate. They have forgotten how to request little perks. Our hurried, stressful, busy lives are unquestionably the most dangerous enemy of celebrating life itself.

"Somehow, we must learn how to achieve momentary slowdowns, and request from God a heightened awareness of the conception that life is a happy thing, a festival to be enjoyed rather than a drudgery to be endured. Life is *full* of perks if we train our souls to perceive them, a thousand tiny things from which one can weave a bright necklace of pleasure for one's life."[1]

So celebrate!

THE WILL TO LIVE FULLY

Welcoming All That Life Offers

Praise our God, O peoples,
  let the sound of his praise be heard;
he has preserved our lives
  and kept our feet from slipping.
For you, O God, tested us;
  you refined us like silver.
You brought us into prison
  and laid burdens on our backs.
You let men ride over our heads;
  we went through fire and water,
  but you brought us to a place of abundance.

—Psalm 66:8–12

As a new believer, Chris suffered a deeply disappointing setback that shook up his faith. "So much so," he told me, "that I felt like chucking it all and returning to my pagan lifestyle. I remember calling up my atheistic friends—friends I'd broken off with because of their negative influence on me—and pouring out my heart to them."

"You know, there's always room for you back here," one of them said to Chris.

It sounded tempting to Chris, but the comment also disturbed him. Not long before, he had told this friend about Christ's power to change lives. How could Chris now contradict everything he'd said?

Chris continued his story: "Around this time, I traveled to London, feeling depressed and confused and desperate for spiritual direction. During this trip, I happened to attend a gathering where Juan Masis, a Spanish existentialist who'd converted to Christianity, preached about Peter's denial of Christ. Masis developed a metaphor I'll never forget. Explaining how Peter denied Christ while standing with nonbelievers around an open fire, Masis said it may feel 'warm' to return to the world's companionship, but eventually we'll get burned."

Chris took the warning to heart.

"Through the years, when I've felt spiritually discouraged, I've remembered this preacher's words," he explained. "I'm reminded that the world can't offer what I need, and it keeps me moving ahead with God instead of going back." With this decision Chris affirmed that with God he could embrace *all* that life offers, not just the good times.

"Better to face all of it with God than without him," he concluded.

To live fully and openly and spiritually, we accept all that affronts us—the drudgery and excitements, disappointments and triumphs—with the assurance God will carry us through. And that is cause to celebrate. Even when we don't feel happy, we can learn to seize the celebratory moments.

Luci Swindoll, an author who writes about enjoying life, gives this advice about celebrating the present: "To experience happiness we must train ourselves to live in this moment, to savor it for what it is, not running ahead in anticipation of some future date or lagging behind in the paralysis of the past.

"'But what if I don't like the here and now?' you ask. 'What if my present moment is one of disappointment or impairment or heartache? How then do I savor the moment?' Good questions. And the answers reside in the first and most profound principle in the art of savoring life. *Pleasure lies in the heart, not in the happenstance.* Our circumstances may be dreadful and riddled with reasons for discouragement and sorrow, but that doesn't mean those moments are utterly devoid of happiness."[2]

Do we dare believe her?

For the sake of our souls, we dare to believe and celebrate.

Lord, I celebrate the ways you've helped, rescued, and loved me in the past. I celebrate this moment, too, with the knowledge of your goodness and joy of your presence. I dare to believe and celebrate my life. I dare to believe and celebrate you!

SPONTANEITY
Cherishing the Moments

Praise the LORD.
Sing to the LORD a new song,
his praise in the assembly of the saints.
Let Israel rejoice in their Maker;
let the people of Zion be glad in their King.
Let them praise his name with dancing
and make music to him with tambourine
and harp.
For the LORD takes delight in his people;
he crowns the humble with salvation.
Let the saints rejoice in this honor
and sing for joy on their beds. . . .
Praise the LORD.

—Psalm 149:1–5, 9

The Old Testament book of Psalms speaks deeply to me because it both laments and celebrates life. On days I'm discouraged, I find comfort; on days I'm elated, I'm told to dance and make music; but most of all I appreciate the psalms because they're spontaneous expressions of the soul.

Spontaneity. We don't use that word much. We prefer our planned programs, printed-up prayers, and standardized teaching notes. Sometimes we forget that spontaneity—doing the unexpected and imaginative—also feeds the soul. To remind myself of this, I keep a greeting card, "How to Be an Artist," tacked above my desk. Sark, the author and artist, suggests that to be spontaneous I do the following:

- stay loose
- learn to watch snails
- plant impossible gardens
- invite someone dangerous to tea
- make little signs that say yes! and post them all over your house
- make friends with freedom and uncertainty
- look forward to dreams
- cry during movies
- swing as high as you can on a swing set, by moonlight
- cultivate moods
- refuse to "be responsible"
- do it for love
- take lots of naps
- give money away
- do it now, the money will follow
- believe in magic
- laugh a lot
- celebrate every gorgeous moment
- take moonbaths
- have wild imaginings, transformative dreams, and perfect calm
- draw on the walls
- read every day
- imagine yourself magic
- giggle with children
- listen to old people
- open up

- dive in
- be free
- bless yourself
- drive away fear
- play with everything
- entertain your inner child
- build a fort
- get wet
- hug trees
- write love letters[3]

Do these suggestions sound "unspiritual" to you? If so, I challenge you to rethink your definition of soul development. Nurturing the woman within isn't all seriousness and discipline; it's also laughter and cutting loose, freeing ourselves to enjoy and be silly. Consequently, I think of these suggestions as full of soul, celebratory, and a means to be childlike before God. (Did you know he asks us to become as children?)

My current favorite suggestion is "celebrate every gorgeous moment," because I've already "planted impossible gardens," "taken lots of naps," and "invited someone dangerous to tea." But I'm also working my way toward "taking moonbaths" and "hugging a tree."

It may be years before I do it, but if I could run into the night (with my robe on, of course) and hug that mangy old oak tree in the backyard, my neighbors might think I'm crazy, but I'd know my soul was free. And I'd feel less afraid of an invisible and spontaneous Lord saying, "Follow me."

God, here is my spontaneous expression to you: I love you! I love you! I love you!

REPEAT ENGAGEMENTS
Securing the Soul Through Ritual

How lovely is your dwelling place,
    O LORD Almighty!
My soul yearns, even faints,
    for the courts of the LORD;
my heart and my flesh cry out
    for the living God. . . .
Blessed are those who dwell in your house;
    they are ever praising you. . . .
Better is one day in your courts
    than a thousand elsewhere;
I would rather be a doorkeeper in the house
        of my God
    than dwell in the tents of the wicked.

—Psalm 84:1–2, 4, 10

Charette likes to eat breakfast by candlelight. She doesn't turn the meal into a big production; she has no time or inclination for that. My friend simply lights a candle to accompany her toast or cereal; it's her private ritual to celebrate a new day.

When Charette told me about her minor celebration, my heart leaped. Something about small rituals stirs me. Amid life's stresses and perplexities, they provide touchstones to remember who we are and what really matters. They secure the soul.

I didn't grow up in a liturgical church, and as a child of the peace-and-love generation, I eschewed anything that appeared ritualistic or traditional. This resulted in my selecting china and silverware patterns at midlife, after finally hungering for what's lasting and familiar. Something about aging transformed me. I hope I'm always open to growing, trying new things, and embarking on adventures, but contrary to my know-it-all youthful thinking, I believe that stability and stimulation can coexist. Ritual anchors us within so we can risk.

Ritual also resides in God's heart. The Bible is full of instructions to God's people about keeping traditions and honoring him as their source and touchstone. As the Israelites approached the temple to worship, as the priest sacrificed unblemished lambs for atonement, as the youth of Israel joyfully danced in the streets, God's children remembered his love and provision for them. Yet meaningful ritual extended beyond public displays and into everyday life. Breaking the bread, drinking the wine, and repeating ancestral stories celebrated God's goodness and filled their souls in simple ways. And these simplicities were probably what children remembered and parents cherished most.

In *The Book of Family Prayer,* Robert E. Webber graces us with small celebrations for the festive seasons of the year—Advent, Christmas, Easter, Pentecost—but what draws me into this book are the "Readings for the Nonfestive Season." He doesn't lead us to celebrate only life's big events; he helps create ritual for ordinary days, too.

Webber explains, "Most of us do not have a ready way to integrate our faith into the events of our lives." This is what his book of prayer is about, but this too is the meaning of ritual. He says, "A ritual—a religious ritual—[has the] power to unite a family, recall history, create reverential awe, shape values and provide a focal point . . . to which memory will return again and again."[4]

Rituals can be just as meaningful for individuals, circles of friends, and work groups as for families; and they aren't always overtly "religious." I've a few friends who, as recovering alcoholics, celebrate their sobriety not only once a year but every day. "We've learned to live one day at a time, to enjoy each day as it comes. We've learned to celebrate in small ways," they tell me. This is the heartbeat of ritual.

If you're interested in creating ritual, in providing a secure place for the soul, you can start in small ways. If you've pondered this book day by day or kept a regular journal, you've already begun. Tomorrow when you read or write, you can light a candle, and you'll be on your way.

Creator God, thank you for your gift of ritual and celebration. Through small and creative remembrances, I want to honor you as my source and touchstone.

REVIVING HOSPITALITY

Gathering Together Our Souls

How good and pleasant it is
when brothers live together in unity!
It is like precious oil poured on the head,
running down on the beard,
running down on Aaron's beard,
down upon the collar of his robes.
It is as if the dew of Hermon
were falling on Mount Zion.
For there the LORD bestows his blessing,
even life forevermore.

—Psalm 133

In a stirring poem, Karen Burton Mains reminds us that hospitality is a gathering together of souls, a gathering we should not miss.

Lord,
Thank You for having given Yourself in intimate,
inexplicable hospitality.
You have been the Host to all creation.

Without dwelling, You have contained the
whole world and inhabited Yourself in the winds,

the corners, and the depths, inviting us to be
at home with You. Beneath the shadow of Your
wing You bid us hide, and in the depths of Your
Being You shelter and refuge us.

Without meat You have nourished us.
Without beverage You have refreshed us.
By Your very Word came sustenance.
On bread and water without price we have been fed.
You have been manna in the wilderness of our lives.

Without a table You have banqueted us,
inviting us, yea, to be married to You.
Over our heads flies the banner of Your love.
We are entertained with the mysteries of faith,
the songs of the Spirit, holy laughter.
You have garmented us in festal righteousness.

As we wandered in wastelands,
You sought us before we called.
You extended eager welcome
though we scarcely knocked.
You embraced us when we were filthy
and oppressed and undeserving.

You are the Samaritan who passes not by,
Who finds lodging for us in the warm inns by the way.
You bake fish over coals, waiting for us,
though we have forgotten to wait for You.
With broken hands You break the loaf of blessing.
Those same wounds caress our leprous spirits.
You do not fear to openly accept the intimate worship
of our harlot hearts.

You are the Host of all mankind.
Lifted up, suffering, with breath, You yet

extend greeting to all the masses,
  "Come unto me . . .
    come . . .
      come . . ."

You give us the mystery of Your presence
in this supper of the ages, this remembrance of
Your ultimate hospitality.

O Lord,
Make my hospitality as unto Yours.
Be forever my archetype of endeavor,
My firstfruit of harvested goodness:
Love for the battered, misused child,
Grace to bind running ulcers of flesh and soul,
Eagerness for the wealthy without servility,
And for the poor without superiority.

Through eternity You have been and will be
utterly hospitable.
Help me
poor, faltering, unfeeling me,
to be like You,

with breath-beat and soul-heart
poured out
emptied
opened.
Help me,
to be given to hospitality.[5]

Lord, prompt me to celebrate by gathering together souls to love one another and reflect your grace. May we dwell in unity and serve you as one. Help me to be given to hospitality.

POSITIVE EXPECTATIONS
About Forgetting the Past

Sing joyfully to the LORD, you righteous;
it is fitting for the upright to praise him.
Praise the LORD with the harp;
make music to him on the ten-stringed lyre.
Sing to him a new song;
play skillfully, and shout for joy.
For the word of the LORD is right and true;
he is faithful in all he does.
The LORD loves righteousness and justice;
the earth is full of his unfailing love.

—Psalm 33:1–5

The English essayist and Christian apologist G. K. Chesterton was brilliant—and absentminded.

Chesterton was an enormous man, and because of his size, he splashed floods of water on the floor while lumbering in and out of the bathtub. Accordingly, the family's maid usually waited outside the bathroom door for him to finish bathing and then hurried in to wipe up when he emerged from the room. If she missed this opportunity, water seeped through the ceiling below.

One day the maid heard Chesterton pull himself out of the tub only to splash back in again. After a momentary pause he groaned, "Oh, no, I've been in here before."

Another time, his wife, Frances, received the cryptic telegram: *Am at Market Harborough. Where should I be?* Frances shook her head and directed him home. She loved him anyway.

Despite his genius and creativity, Chesterton could forget. Spiritually, we could benefit from the great writer's example. We're better off forgetting the past and pressing forward even if we don't always know where we're going. Living in the past and fueling regret strangles the soul.

The Bible teaches us not only to forget the past but to celebrate the future. The book of Proverbs promises, "Do not let your heart envy sinners, but always be zealous for the fear of the LORD. There is surely a future hope for you, and your hope will not be cut off. . . . Know also that wisdom is sweet to your soul; if you find it, there is a future hope for you, and your hope will not be cut off."

God told the prophet Isaiah, "Forget the former things; do not dwell on the past. See, I am doing a new thing! Now it springs up; do you not perceive it? I am making a way in the desert and streams in the wasteland."

"'For I know the plans I have for you,' declares the LORD, 'plans to prosper you and not to harm you, plans to give you hope and a future. Then you will call upon me and come and pray to me, and I will listen to you. You will seek me and find me when you seek me with all your heart.'"

The apostle Paul wrote, "But one thing I do: Forgetting what is behind and straining toward what is ahead, I press on toward the goal to win the prize for which God has called me heavenward in Christ Jesus. All of us who are mature should take such a view of things. And if on some point you think differently, that too God will make clear to you."

Forgetting the past. Hoping in the future. Celebrating the day in between.

These are the positive expectations of Scripture.

These are what secure and shape a woman's soul.

Glorious God, thank you for forgetting my past and ushering me into the future with your hope. For these, I celebrate!

NOTES

PART ONE—Hiding: *Pulling Away and Within*

1. Alice Slaikeu Lawhead, *The Lie of the Good Life* (Portland, Ore.: Multnomah Press, 1989), 10.

2. Clifton Fadiman, ed., *The Little, Brown Book of Anecdotes* (Boston: Little, Brown and Company, 1985), 5.

3. Larry Crabb, *Inside Out* (Colorado Springs: NavPress, 1988), 14.

4. Lewis Carroll, *Adventures in Wonderland and Through the Looking-Glass* (New York: New American Library of World Literature, 1960), 144–45.

5. "Under His Wings" by William O. Cushing and Ira D. Sankey. *Crusader Hymns* (Chicago: Hope, 1967), 195.

6. Annie Dillard, *Holy the Firm* (New York: Harper & Row, 1977), 19, 24.

7. Richard J. Foster, *Celebration of Discipline* (San Francisco: Harper & Row, 1978), 84.

8. Angela Partington, ed., *The Oxford Dictionary of Quotations,* vol. 4 (New York: Oxford Univ. Press, 1992), n.p.

9. A. W. Tozer, *The Price of Neglect* (Camp Hill, Pa.: Christian Publications, 1991), 22–23.

10. Andrew Murray, *Waiting on God* (Fort Washington, Pa.: Christian Literature Crusade, 1995), 105.

PART TWO—Resting: *Leaning on Everlasting Arms*

1. *Webster's New World Dictionary,* Second College Edition, s.v. "rest."

2. Information retrieved from the World Wide Web: http://www.nettips.com/sleep/homepage.html. Sponsored by Select Comfort Air Sleep Systems, February 1996.

3. Frederick Buechner, *The Magnificent Defeat* (San Francisco: Harper & Row, 1966), 17–18. Used by permission.

PART THREE—Cleansing: *Restoring the Inner Person*

1. "God Betwixt Me," *The Quiet Hour* (September-November 1988), 19.

2. "Nothing Between" by C. A. Tindley. *Hymns of the Christian Life* (Harrisburg, Pa.: Christian Publications, 1936), 449.

3. Karl Menninger, *Whatever Became of Sin?* (New York: E. P. Dutton, 1974), 1–2.

4. Richard Foster, *Celebration of Discipline: The Path to Spiritual Growth* (San Francisco: HarperSanFrancisco, 1988), 130–31.

5. Sharon Wegscheider-Cruse, "Without Forgiveness, There Can Be No Hope," *National Catholic Reporter* (October 28, 1989), n.p.

6. Bert Ghezzi, *Transforming Problems* (Ann Arbor, Mich.: Servant Publications, 1986), 32.

7. Mary Catherine Bateson, *Composing a Life* (New York: Atlantic Monthly Press, 1989), 53–54.

8. Bateson, *Composing a Life,* 40.

PART FOUR—Surrendering: *Giving All to a Generous God*

1. Fadiman, *The Little, Brown Book of Anecdotes,* 28.

2. Dietrich Bonhoeffer, *The Cost of Discipleship* (New York: Macmillan, 1961), 211–12.

3. A. W. Tozer, *This World: Playground or Battleground?* (Camp Hill, Pa.: Christian Publications, 1989), 120–21.

4. Partington, *The Oxford Dictionary of Quotations,* 12.

PART FIVE—Seeking: *Meeting God in Prayer*

1. Catherine Marshall, *Adventures in Prayer* (Old Tappan, N.J.: Chosen, 1975), 7–9. Used by permission.

2. Andrew Murray, *The Believer's Prayer Life* (Minneapolis: Bethany House, 1983), 107–8.

3. Frank S. Mead, ed., *The Encyclopedia of Religious Quotations* (Old Tappan, N.J.: Revell, 1965), 340.

4. Fadiman, *The Little, Brown Book of Anecdotes,* 522–23.

5. Mead, *The Encyclopedia of Religious Quotations,* 344.

6. Paris Reidhead, *Beyond Petition* (Minneapolis: Bethany Fellowship, 1974), 38.

7. Andrew Murray, *The Secret of Adoration* (Fort Washington, Pa.: Christian Literature Crusade, 1979), 20–21.

PART SIX—Hearing: *Listening to His Voice*

1. Robert Siegel, *Whalesong* (Westchester, Ill.: Crossway, 1981), 14.

2. Hannah Whitall Smith, *Daily Devotions from the Christian's Secret of a Happy Life* (Old Tappan, N.J.: Revell, 1984), 87, 89. Used by permission.

3. C. S. Lewis, *The Problem of Pain* (New York: Macmillan, 1977), 93.

4. Flannery O'Connor, *A Good Man Is Hard to Find and Other Stories* (New York: Harcourt, Brace Javonovich, 1976), 193–96.

5. Judith Couchman, "Ministry of the Ears: The Listening Evangelism," *Adult Creative Teaching Aids,* Lesson 2, December 11 (Elgin, Ill.: David C. Cook, 1983), 1–6. Used by permission of the author.

PART SEVEN—Reflecting: *Developing a Discerning Mind*

1. Fadiman, *The Little, Brown Book of Anecdotes,* 523.

2. Fadiman, *The Little, Brown Book of Anecdotes,* 522.

3. Jane Brody, *Jane Brody's Good Food Book* (New York: Norton & Company, 1985), 39–40.

4. Fadiman, *The Little, Brown Book of Anecdotes,* 104.

5. Joy Gage, *Every Woman's Privilege* (Portland, Ore.: Multnomah Press, 1986), 33–34.

6. Bonhoeffer, *The Cost of Discipleship,* 41.

7. John Bartlett, ed., *Familiar Quotations* (Boston: Little, Brown and Company, 1980), 552.

PART EIGHT—Seeing: *Looking Past the Physical World*

1. Fadiman, *The Little, Brown Book of Anecdotes,* 360.

2. Mead, *The Encyclopedia of Religious Quotations,* 464.

3. Catherine Marshall, ed., *The Prayers of Peter Marshall* (Lincoln, Va.: Chosen, 1954), 166. Used by permission.

4. Madame Guyon, *Madame Guyon: An Autobiography* (Chicago: Moody Press, n.d.), 381–82.

5. From the introduction to *Madame Guyon: An Autobiography,* 5.

6. Randall M. Miller and Linda Patterson Miller, eds., *The Book of American Diaries* (New York: Avon, 1995), 400.

7. Amy Carmichael, *Rose from Brier* (Fort Washington, Pa.: Christian Literature Crusade, 1995), 33.

8. Marshall, *Adventures in Prayer,* 17. Used by permission.

PART NINE—Being: *Placing the Value on Character*

1. Fadiman, *The Little, Brown Book of Anecdotes,* 169.

2. Mead, *The Encyclopedia of Religious Quotations,* 206.

3. Phil Cousineau, ed., *Soul: An Archaeology* (San Francisco: Harper & Row, 1994), 47. "The Physicians" is an adaptation of a traditional folktale by Paul Jordan Smith, published in *Parabola, The Magazine of Myth and Tradition,* vol. III, no. 1.

4. "Hard Hearts," *The Quiet Hour* (April-June 1988), n.p.

5. This philosophy is credited to D'Arcy Wentworth Thompson.

6. Rebecca Manley Pippert, *Hope Has Its Reasons* (San Francisco: Harper & Row, 1989), 131.

7. D. Patrick Miller, *A Little Book of Forgiveness* (New York: Viking, 1994), n.p.

8. Gurney Williams III, "Hopping—Heart Stopping—Mad," *Longevity* (August 1994), n.p.

PART TEN—Loving: *Sharing the Soul with Others*

1. Fadiman, *The Little, Brown Book of Anecdotes,* 502.

2. Thomas Moore, *Soul Mates* (New York: Harper Perennial, 1994), 94.

3. Alan Boubil and Claude-Michel Schonberg, "Finale," *Les Misérables Broadway Album,* Geffen Records, 1987.

4. *Aesop's Fables* (n.p.: Grosset & Dunlap, 1947), 18.

5. Mead, *The Encyclopedia of Religious Quotations,* 331.

6. John White, *The Fight* (Downers Grove, Ill.: InterVarsity Press, 1976), 15–16.

PART ELEVEN—**Serving:** ***Doing What Grows the Soul***

1. Mead, *The Encyclopedia of Religious Quotations,* 403.

2. Mead, *The Encyclopedia of Religious Quotations,* 26.

3. Mother Teresa's prayer, "Words to Love by" © 1983 Ave Maria Press, Notre Dame, IN as quoted in *Seeking the Heart of God* (San Francisco: Harper & Row, 1993), 52–53.

4. Alexandr Solzhenitsyn, *A World Split Apart* (New York: Harper & Row, 1978), 17–19.

5. Mother Teresa and Brother Roger, *Seeking the Heart of God,* 18–19.

PART TWELVE—**Celebrating:** ***Rejoicing in Each Day***

1. Luci Swindoll, *Celebrating Life* (Colorado Springs: NavPress, 1989), 11–12. Used by permission of NavPress.

2. Luci Swindoll, *You Bring the Confetti* (Dallas: Word, 1986), 17. Used by permission.

3. The card is published by Red Rose, P.O. Box 280140, San Francisco, CA 94128. 1–800–374–5505. © 1993 Sark. Used by permission of the artist.

4. Robert E. Webber, *The Book of Family Prayer* (Nashville: Nelson, 1986), 19, 15.

5. Karen Burton Mains, *Open Heart, Open Home* (Elgin, Ill.: David C. Cook, 1976), 197–99. Used by permission of the author.

We want to hear from you. Please send your comments about this book to us in care of the address below. Thank you.

ZondervanPublishingHouse
Grand Rapids, Michigan 49530
http://www.zondervan.com